BEAUTIFUL ASHES

Finding Freedom Through Faith

Student Addition

SHELLEY FURTADO-LINTON

Beautiful Ashes Publishing Group
Sioux Falls, SD

DEDICATION

This book is dedicated to my grandkids. You are fearfully and wonderfully made, and I'm blessed to watch you grow, and see how God will use each one of you!

I'm also grateful and inspired by the strong, funny, challenging, and capable young women I've met along the way. You are the inspiration for this book and the reason I do what I do.

Thank you for being who you are. As you read this book, I pray you will find your voice and grab hold of the identity God created for you.

TABLE OF CONTENTS

INTRODUCTION

Everything we do is filtered through the experiences we have in life. If we are alive, we are going to experience a mix of happy and sad things. Whether the things we go through are something we brought on ourselves, or something that someone else did to us, our life experiences shape us. The good and bad things we go through mix together, can impact us in big ways, and many times, shape how we see ourselves.

Some moments are happy or fun, like winning the championship game, traveling somewhere amazing for a vacation, or getting that special thing that you've wanted for a very long time.

Those experiences end up become memories we look back on with joy later in life. But even smaller pleasures like laughing over a cup of coffee, sharing a favorite meal, or hearing a favorite song become part of who we are.

In this life, most of us can be sure we will have at least a bit of happiness. But, usually, everyone also has hard things to face.

Maybe someone you love passes away, your parents get divorced, or an important relationship ends. We all have sad and happy times. Some days it feels like we're up on the mountaintop, and others it feels like we are down in the desert.

Whatever the experiences we have, one thing is true; whether good or bad, everything we go through combines to create the story of our lives.

> *Ecclesiastes 7:14*
> When times are good, be happy; but when times are bad, consider this: God has made the one as well as the other.

Sometimes, though, it seems as though our lives bring more bad experiences than good. What happens when someone has more heartbreak, trauma, hurt, and pain than joy and happiness? How do the hard things that happen affect us?

When it seems like there is nothing but hard in our lives, can we still have hope?

Yes, I believe we can. I *know* there is always hope because I've personally experienced what happens when God reshapes the messages that life gives us. He can fix our brokenness, help us figure out who we are, and change the direction of our lives.

Introduction

Just like in the scripture in Isaiah 61:3, He promises to take the heartbreaking, broken, and burned things in our lives and replace it all with a beautiful story.

The experiences I had growing up could have defined me. But God's love transformed me, changed where I was headed, and shaped me into who I am today. Just like it says in chapter eight of Romans, God is working all of it together for good in my life.

It's amazing that God would choose to use broken people like me, but He does. It makes me so happy to share this good news with you.

> *Jeremiah 29:11*
> "For I know the plans I have for you," declares the Lord, "plans to prosper you and not to harm you, plans to give you hope and a future."

Know that no matter where you are today, there is hope and a beautiful future for you! I believe this with my whole heart – even if you don't just yet.

My prayer is that God will use His word, and my story, to heal your heart and to help you grow closer to Him. The journey from brokenness to hope is not always easy. It takes time, and determination, but it's completely worth it!

God created you with a purpose and an identity. He promises to make you whole, and the first step starts here.

Will you join me? Let's walk this out together.

CHAPTER ONE – THE POOL

The Story

I love books… especially ones where the underdog wins! You know, the ones that tell real stories of people who struggle, fall, and then, against all odds, find hope and healing, and rise up to triumph!

The Bible is full of those stories. In scripture, you'll find people who are good, bad, weak, strong, whole, and broken. New and Old Testament stories include tragedies, love stories, mysteries, and history. And every word provides a glimpse into who people are, and how they think and feel.

There are many Bible stories where people overcome terrible situations, and find victory. There are so many wonderful accounts of lives where restoration and healing happen.

Every one of those stories is inspiring.

We can all find someone in those stories to relate to. But there's one specific Bible story that I am drawn to. I believe this particular story is a good example of what happens when people get stuck because of things that have happened in their lives. I believe anyone who has ever been stuck will be able to relate.

The story I'm talking about is the one about the man at the pool of Bethesda that's talked about in John 5:1-15. If you aren't familiar with the story, let me tell you about it.

This event took place during the time that Jesus lived. The people in that area believed the Bethesda pool could heal the sick. This specific story revolves around a man who had been coming there for many years, hoping that he too could be cured.

We're told he's been lame for thirty-eight years, but we don't know what his specific "lameness" is. He probably had a physical problem, but it's also possible he had a spiritual or emotional issue. We don't know for sure, and it doesn't matter because there are many ways, we humans can be broken.

In the story, we are told this guy's been lying by that pool for a very long time. We find out he goes there every day hoping to be healed. It's fascinating because, we don't know how he's been getting there.

He couldn't have lived there, and he was lame, so how was he getting from his home to the pool?

Did friends or family bring him? Obviously, he was pretty determined.

What's clear is that he's serious enough about getting healed that he gets himself there day after day.

Interesting, right? Nobody does something day after day unless they expect to get something out of it. I think this is a clue that this guy probably wanted his life to be different.

The thing is, just like this guy, many of us suffer from some type of lameness. Sure, we could be physically lame. The truth is we can be "disabled" in a lot of other ways. Maybe we struggle with depression, or anxiety, or emotional brokenness.

Maybe we're paralyzed by fear. Maybe we are held captive by negative thoughts or emotions. Whatever it is, if it's causing us to miss out on the life God promises us, it's lameness.

No doubt, our experiences can impact us, and the bad things that happen can sideline us. Sometimes we are able to move past difficult stuff that happens. But every so often, the difficult experiences from our past or present get us stuck so deeply it can seem like there's no way out.

Sometimes things happen and it seems as though we just can't get past them. When that happens, we get stuck, lose hope, and can't move forward into God's plan for our lives.

Remember this… Whatever negative thing holds onto you, holds you back.

Back to our story. One day, while our friend at the pool of Bethesda is lying there on his mat, Jesus walks up and asks him if he wants to be healed. Can you picture that? What was that like? By the time this happened, Jesus was pretty well known, so this guy probably had heard about him.

Think about meeting some famous person you've been a fan of for a long time….

Was he calm, or did he freak out a bit?

How would you react if Jesus showed up in person and offered to heal you? I've always thought if Jesus asked me a question like that, I wouldn't hesitate to say, "Yes, yes, yes, please!"

More than likely our lame friend probably knew about the miracles Jesus preformed. So, what the man does when Jesus offers to heal him is very strange.

Jesus offers to help, but Instead of taking advantage of the offer, our guy simply explains to Jesus why he can't be healed.

He mentions that in all the years he's come to the pool, no one has helped to get him into the water. He tells Jesus that other people have been healed because they've gotten in before him. He has a lot of excuses about why he *hasn't* been healed, but he never does answer Jesus' question about whether he *wants* to be healed.

Again, this seems weird.

Remember, this guy's been pretty committed to going to the pool every day. He knows it's a place of healing, so it's pretty clear he probably wants to be healed. So why not tell Jesus he wants to get better?

What happens next is even more curious. Jesus doesn't do what we (or maybe the man?) expect him to do. He really doesn't actually heal the guy. He doesn't rub mud on the man, or lay hands on him. Jesus doesn't carry him into the healing water, and he never actually says, "Be healed."

No. Jesus just tells the man to 'pick up his mat and walk.' Wow. Just a simple command and the man stands up and walks. That's all it took after thirty-eight years of waiting for a miracle!

It seems so simple, and it's easy to skim over what actually happened in this story. At first glance, it doesn't seem significant, until we look closer.

When we do, we see that, like many Bible stories, there's a lot more to it. There is so much to learn from the details in this guy's story. And friends… it's *all* in the details.

To start with, the name of the pool, Bethesda, means "grace and mercy." Bethesda is more than a pretty name – it's a powerful name and those words prove it!

You see, grace means we get the kindness of God, even though we can't earn it and don't deserve it. It's like getting a very extravagant gift we were not expecting, can't pay for, and did nothing to earn. Getting what you *don't* deserve – that's grace.

Mercy is different. It means having compassion or forgiveness for someone who deserves to be punished. If you committed an awful crime, and were scheduled to be executed, but were let go even though you were guilty, that would be mercy. *Not* getting what you deserve – that's mercy.

Together, grace and mercy describe salvation. Look at what the apostle Paul says about that in his letter to the Jewish Christians who lived in Jerusalem.

> *Hebrews 4:16*
> Let us then approach God's throne of grace with confidence, so that we may receive mercy and find grace to help us in our time of need.

He's talking about the gospel message of salvation!

The good news of the gospel is that even when we were still sinners, God sent His only son to pay the penalty for us.

> *Romans 5:8*
> But God demonstrates his own love for us in this:
> While we were still sinners, Christ died for us.

That is grace and mercy, and that is redemption.

Think about it. It means this man was only a few feet away from his own redemption!

Still, it's interesting that for all those years, he stayed right there on the edge. He went there every day, which makes me think he did have a little hope.

But for some reason, just couldn't make the short journey from mat to water.

Sadly, his whole life had revolved around his lameness. And "lameness" had become his identity. He was "the lame guy by the pool."

Every day for years and years, he went to the edge of healing pool, but never actually got in. It's pretty clear, he was stuck.

It seems silly when we think about it, but can we really blame him?

I believe if we're honest, we can agree that we get stuck, too. We want things to be different. We may even try to change. But we end up in the same place we've always been.

I can totally relate to this guy. I know what it's like to want a different life, but feel like nothing is ever going to change. I've been stuck. There was a time I wanted change, but I had spent such a long time trapped in a bad place, I didn't know how to make my life different.

What's funny about this is, I'd read this scripture many times, and never thought twice about this guy. But I'd been asking God to help me find something that would inspire and challenge the people in my small group study.

I'd spend a lot of time in prayer, but it was on a flight to the happiest place on earth – thirty-thousand feet above the earth – when the words jumped off the page for me.

At first, I tried to skip past the verses, but I kept coming back to them. I felt the Lord nudging me to use the story, but I hesitated. The story of the man at the pool didn't seem very exciting or interesting. I really didn't think this was the right story for my Bible study friends.

Still, I could definitely relate to the guy. It made perfect sense to me. I could totally understand why he would go to the pool every day hoping to receive healing. And I understood why he laid down right next to the pool of grace and mercy, wanting so badly to be healed, and yet having no clue how to make it happen.

Yep, I completely understood this guy.

I wasn't sure anyone else would be able to relate, but eventually, I began to understand that a lot of us get stuck in our beliefs, in our brokenness, and in our habits. Life can be really hard, and trouble and heartache can break even the strongest person.

There was a time in my life when I laid by my own mat.

Bad things from my childhood had damaged me, and that damage had impacted every part of my life – from the relationships I had, to choices I made. The experiences I'd had changed how I saw the world, and, most of all how, I saw myself.

Growing up, I'd had some really bad stuff happen. Those experiences caused brokenness. Just like this guy in the story, at some point, I got stuck, and stayed stuck for a long time.

I wanted to be healed, and I wanted my life to be different. But the truth was, I had no idea how change could happen.

Just like the man on the mat, I thought the healing pool was just too unreachable.

Your Pool of Bethesda

Over time, I started to understand that the words in John 5:1-15 described my story. Just like that guy, I had also been trapped in a mess and thought things could never be different.

Looking back, I could see how I let my past convince me that my life could never change.

Sitting in that airplane, reading the words in those verses, I was in a good place. At first, it was hard to see how they were related to my own healing journey. But even then, I began to understand how important this guy's story is.

I knew the journey I had been on was a lot like the man at the pool.

I knew there were many other people who had similar stories. So, I started to take a look at what had gotten me from the mat to the pool.

The changes in my life began with a good hard look in the mirror.

The first thing I did was to identify where I was broken and how I had gotten stuck. Look, we can't change without looking at our own lives. Change only happens when we acknowledge what's not working.

If you want your life to be different, you have to take this step, too. So, I'm going to ask you be honest with yourself. What's not working in your own life?

Sometimes it's hard to know when we are broken, but there are some things that may reveal where you could use some help.

Here are some ways you can tell if you need healing. Ask yourself, if you:

- Look at yourself as damaged or defective.
- Make poor decisions because of how you see yourself.
- Speak badly or negatively to yourself.
- Don't believe God can fix you.
- Can't imagine a life without sadness or pain.

If you answered "yes" to *any* of these questions, then there's probably some things that need to change. And it's okay, because we all have things that need to change, so there's a good chance you are in good company.

We start by looking at ourselves, because change always starts with admitting where we are.

But listen, everyone's journey is unique, so don't compare your wounds with anyone else's. It doesn't matter how deep the cut is, or how long it's been there. If it's making you lame, it's time for it to change.

In our story, Jesus asked the man if he wanted to be healed.

Are you ready to answer that question for yourself? You'll know it's time if you've been stuck in the same place for a long time, you're doing the same thing over and over, or, if what you believe is keeping you from moving on or moving up. Whatever it is, if you're here, it's time to get up off the mat you're on.

It's important to look at what's going on in our lives right now. Like I said before, healing begins when we accept where we are *today*.

We have to be honest, and that means we need to be brave as we try to figure out how we ended up stuck on a mat, only a few feet from the pool of grace and mercy.

I know this process can seem very big and scary, but be courageous. Let yourself settle in while we walk through the process.

I am confident that with God's help, you can get to a place of healing.

While we don't know what caused the man in chapter five of John to become lame, we do know it kept him stuck. Maybe he didn't think he would ever be healed, but kept coming close to the waters of Bethesda every day anyway.

Somewhere deep inside him, there had to have been a little spark of hope.

He may have been stuck, but he didn't give up, and you shouldn't either. No matter how long you've been where you are, there's every reason to believe your future can be different.

So... Will you take this journey with me? It's okay if it's uncomfortable or scary. We'll walk through this together. I promise you, it'll be worth it.

Questions

Acknowledging where we are today is a big part of healing. There are a lot of ways we can be lame, but we can recognize it because it limits us physically, mentally, emotionally, or spiritually.

Take a moment now to identify your own "lameness."

1. What are some ways the experiences you've had have caused you to become "lame?"

2. In what ways has your "lameness" caused problems in your life, or held you back?

3. What is one way you've become stuck?

CHAPTER TWO – THE BANNER

My Banner

In chapter one of Jeremiah, it says that God set us apart before we were born. This means He created each of us with a unique identity and a specific purpose. It's a wonderful promise, and I believe it is true for me *and* for you.

But the circumstances when I was born, and the experiences I had as a young child damaged the identity God created for me, and it impacted me for a good part of my life.

Growing up, I would describe the world I lived in as terrifying.

My parents were emotionally unhealthy people who met, married, and had a family. My mom had been damaged by the things that had happened in her own family, and she struggled with mental illness for most of her life. The unique and perfect identity that God had designed for *her* had been destroyed by what she experienced growing up.

That damage caused her to have trouble for most of her life and it affected everyone around her.

Her life was a nonstop cycle of drama, fear, anger, and a need to control. She didn't much like being a mom, and she believed one child was enough to handle. So, when she found out that she was pregnant a second time, she was angry. She believed one more child was a problem. And she knew a way to fix it.

She didn't want me, so she made a plan to have an abortion. She made the arrangements, but my dad and his sister found out about it, and they stopped her on her way to the appointment. So, I was born to a mother who did not want me.

Growing up, she made it clear to me that I was a mistake. As long as I can remember, she let me know I was "unwanted." Almost daily she told me how much better her life would have been if she'd been allowed to have the abortion. She often told me she wished I'd never been born.

God had designed me with a purpose He created for me alone. But I heard those words so often, I believed they were the truth. God had given me a unique identity, but her words went deep and began to cause rips in the character He had created for me.

As kids, we tend to believe almost everything we are told.

My mom said I was unwanted, a mistake, and unloved. So, I believed her words were truth. The things she said were believable because she was a grownup, and she was my mom, and she'd never lie... right? Since I thought she was telling the truth, I began to believed her words about me. What she said became a big part of what I believed about myself.

It wasn't just the things she *said* that damaged my identity. There was physical abuse too. Sometimes she'd lock me in the basement for the entire day without food or water.

Other times, she would beat me with a thick leather strap. I was made to kneel on uncooked rice on the hardwood floor until my knees bled. She pulled my hair, pinched my face, and pushed me down. There was no safe place at my house, and the abuse made me fearful and anxious.

The identity God had created for me was damaged in other ways too.

I was only five years old when I was sexually molested by a family member. And it happened a second time by another individual when I was seven. Those experiences taught me I was powerless and had no voice. They taught me I did not have the right to say no. I believed I had to earn love, and that anyone who wanted, had a right to my body.

Soon, I began to see myself through words like shame, dirty, and damaged.

My mother was unpredictable and frightening, but she wasn't the only one who hurt me. My dad also played a part in the abuse. He never touched me sexually. But he was verbally and physically abusive. And even though it happened less than it did with my mom, and was not as harsh than hers, it still happened.

Of everything he did, though, the most damaging was when he ignored what my mom was doing. He did that by working several jobs, and by staying away from home as much as possible.

When he *was* home, he looked away and acted like he didn't know what was going on. He often looked away and pretended he did not see what was happening. He never stopped her, and that taught me I had no value and was not worth saving.

The sexual, verbal, and physical abuse I suffered changed how I saw myself. It made me believe I was a mistake, unwanted, unloved, and had no value. It taught me that no one cared and no one could (or would) save me.

These words, I believed about myself. My beliefs became my identity, and I didn't know how to get past that.

God Given Banners

What I've come to realize is that everything we know about who we are, is tied up in what we believe about ourselves. Our identify plays a big role in how we interact with the world around us.

I believed I was broken, unloved, unwanted, and a mistake, so I behaved like someone who was broken, unloved, unwanted, and a mistake.

I didn't believe my life could be different because I didn't understand my true, God-given identity. It's like a pilot flying a plane without understanding what a plane is or how it works. You can't operate a machine you know nothing about.

One of the biggest roadblocks we have is not understanding who God says we are. And that can keep us from really healing and from becoming who He created us to be. We have to know who we are and who created us.

So, know this…

You were created by a master artist! It's true!!

The same God who fills the night sky with stars and paints the morning sky with the sunrise created you!

You were formed with a unique character, talents, gifts, and abilities all put together by a loving God who designed you with a purpose.

This is so important, friends, because the identity God creates for us becomes our banner.

Let me explain what I mean by "a banner."

Banners are often raised or carried to announce or describe something or someone. They are used to tell everyone who's coming.

Think about this, if a high school band is walking along a parade route without a banner, we'd have no idea who they were. Without a banner, how do you know who or what you are looking at?

Our God-given banners are like that too. The blueprint of our banner tells us – and everyone around us – who we are. And most importantly, we relate to the world around us through our banner.

Banners are what set us apart from everyone else. They define everything about us. They move us through life, and they are our roadmap.

Your banner is so important, it was designed specifically for you before you were born! There is nothing accidental about you, your identify, or your banner!

You are not a random combination of hair, skin, and bones. You are not just a mixture of your parent's DNA. Your life did not happen by chance.

No! You were formed with a purpose, designed long before you came to be.

You see, God creates every one of us with a unique identity that was designed just for us. It describes who we are, what we're like, and it includes things like personality and talents. Every little bit of who we are was designed by our heavenly Father. No part of us is random or accidental, no matter what science might try to tell you. God created a masterpiece when he designed you and me.

And guess what? It says this in scripture too! The Bible has many verses that declare we were formed by God, with a purpose and a one-and-only design. Verse fourteen in Psalm 139 tells us we are uniquely and wonderfully made! According to 1 Peter 2:9 we are chosen by God. Ephesians 2:10 says we're His workmanship. Verse after verse--all confirming the care our Heavenly Father took when He created us. So many verses--all pointing to our individually formed identity.

One of the most incredible things about the way we are designed, is that none of us are alike! You are not like any other human that is, was, or ever will exist. Think about this. No two of us are alike.

Like snowflakes, each one of us is completely different from the next.

It's a remarkable concept, especially when you look out at a blanket of newly fallen snow. Just like that snowflake, your God-created banner is yours and yours alone.

Banners are unique and they are designed to equip us to do what God purposed for our life. Everyone should know who they are, and understanding our banner is an important part of this journey.

So, what is your banner like?

Some banners can be soft and quiet, and some are so big they enter the room before you do. Some are funny. Some are serious. Some prefer to be around large groups of people, while some are happier around one or two friends.

Everyone is different, and no banner is better than another. In verse four of 1 Corinthians chapter twelve it says, even though we all belong to the same God, He created each of us with different kinds of gifts.

One of the best ways to figure out your banner is to take a good look at how others might describe you. If asked, what kind of words would they say?

Would they say you are funny, happy, and easy going, or would they use words like sarcastic and bossy? Silly or serious? Are you the life of the party, or the quiet observer? Are you the musical one, or the one who never knows the words to the song? Are you the sports nut, the gamer, the computer geek?

What makes you...well, YOU?

Broken Banners

As we grow, the banners we are born with can experience some hurt. Life can, and usually does, damage our banners to one degree or another.

Maybe your banner has a chip here or there. Life can be tough, and just about every person has experienced something that has rubbed thin, or made a mark on their banner. Mostly, those markings become life experiences. Many times, they help make us wiser or give us perspective. Those kinds of things usually add beauty and character to the masterpiece God created.

Sometimes, though, the damage is big, and it causes tears in our banner. There are times, when things that happen in life can cause deep gashes and holes. Sometimes life is so bad, and our banners become so broken, they no longer look like the one's God created for us.

When that happens, it can change how we see ourselves. I call those broken banners.

There are a lot of ways our banners can get damaged, and some are worse than others. But the most terrible damage happens when the words we hear and the experiences we have, say things about us that go against what God says, and can change our understanding of who He says we are.

When we don't understand who God says we are, it rips away the identity He created for us. This kind of damage can cause us to make poor choices and go down roads we were never meant to travel.

In one way or another, damage to our banners changes how we see ourselves. The end result when it happens is that we start to see ourselves through a damaged banner. And one thing is clear... damaged banners change us in negative ways.

I'm convinced this is satan's work. It makes sense, since the Bible says he hates God's creation. In 1 Peter 5:8, he's described as a roaring lion roaming around looking for someone to destroy! I believe satan's greatest weapon is destroying the banners God created for us. Once he convinces us we are not who God says we are, it takes very little to keep us broken and stuck.

Recognizing Broken Banners

Whatever experiences or words caused the damage to our banners, there is always hope. However, if we are ever going to heal, we must figure out where our banners are damaged.

Anyone who's worked through their brokenness starts here.

Sometimes the differences between the banner God created for us, and the one that's broken is pretty clear. Some broken banners are just easier to spot than others. For example, if someone is covering up their pain with drugs, alcohol, or promiscuity, they probably have a damaged banner.

If someone is constantly aggressive with everyone around them, or if people describe them as difficult, angry, or troubled, they probably have a damaged banner.

Another way to identify damaged banners is by looking for things that keep us stuck in pain, thoughts of failure, self-hatred, anxiety, hopelessness, anger, or violence. If those things are part of our lives, we're probably experiencing the effects of a broken banner.

When we're making a lot of poor choices, have a string of difficult relationships, or are leaving a trail of trouble everywhere we go, it's easy to see our banner is broken.

Sometimes, though, it's not so easy to put your finger on what is wrong. That's because sometimes the things we're doing seem acceptable. Some of the things we do to feel better, or cover up what's going on inside, may not look "bad." They may even seem positive, or look like success on the surface.

We may look at someone with this type of broken banner and think they look "normal." At first glance, this person may seem like their life is going well. But here's the thing, even though what they are doing looks good on the surface, underneath there's a mess. The problem is what's going on inside. This person does the "right" things, but they are secretly breaking inside.

It's exhausting to hold that kind of messiness down. The person with a broken banner may push what they're feeling down deep inside themselves. But you can't ignore it, or push it away. A person trying to push it all down, often behaves in troubling ways, is depressed, or has anxiety.

Sometimes it's difficult for someone in this situation to keep their broken banner hidden. Sooner or later, it's going to come to the surface.

A lot of times, if they are pushed too far, they'll blow up all over everyone around them, and that's probably going to be an explosion that impacts anyone within striking distance.

Damaged banners can trigger extreme emotions. Look for things like depression, anger, or even rage that are bigger than they should be, or not related to the situation. Everyone gets angry or down from time to time, but these emotions are extreme and often random. If you aren't sure, ask this question. Is the individual being ruled by their emotions? If so, there is probably a broken banner at the heart of it.

Other less obvious broken banners may include behaviors such as being a perfectionist or needing constant control. These may not seem as bad, but make no mistake, they are no less harmful than other broken banners. Grace and mercy are usually for-eign concepts for someone who's a perfectionist. And someone who's always got to be in control does not have room for trust. Without grace, mercy, and trust, we cannot have faith.

Some broken banners can be tricky to spot, and to find them we have to be really honest about what's motivating our actions.

Here are a few things to ask yourself:

- Do I always have to be the best because I'm trying to fill some broken place?
- Have my accomplishments become a way to feel loved?
- Do I get frustrated or angry with myself if I make a mistake?

Sometimes the best way to figure out if you have a broken banner is to take a look at how you feel when you don't win. If failing, making mistakes, or being second, throws you into a bad place, it may mean you have a damaged banner.

This is not a list of every type of broken banner, so if I didn't call out a specific behavior, it doesn't mean it's not an issue.

If you're here, you probably have something to sort out. Remember, if what you believe about yourself does not line up with God's word, it's not your God given banner; it's a false identity.

Unwanted. Mistake. Powerless. Not worth saving. Fearful. Shameful. Dirty. Damaged…

All these words jumbled together to completely obscure my identity. By the time I was a teenager, the banner God had so carefully designed for me was so far gone, it may as well have been burned to ashes.

Everything I did was based on what I believed about myself. I acted out my broken banner because it was my reality. The damage of the words and abuse I had experienced showed up in my life in damaging relationships, self-destructive behavior, and bad choices. Every bit of my life showed I had a broken banner.

There was hardly any part of my life that didn't mirror what I'd learned as a child, and believed about myself. When I was very young, I was frightened and withdrawn. I felt unloved and unwanted. I thought I was a mistake. I believed I had to earn love.

Later in life, I became depressed, anxious, promiscuous, and self-destructive.

I had no boundaries, so I tumbled through a long string of terrible relationships. And every time I did, a little more of my banner was destroyed.

By the time I reached adulthood, my identify was torn, dirty, and really didn't look at all like the one God had created for me. Life looked hopeless because I was viewing it through a very broken banner.

Thankfully, God doesn't see things the way we do. He had a plan for me and nothing He promises can be changed.

The Bible says in 2 Corinthians 1:20 that God always says yes to His promises.

Maybe you are thinking there's no hope for you. I understand that, and it's okay. I didn't know that His promises were real or that His plan was something I could count on. It turns out, God's promises are more than we ever could ask for or imagine.

What I didn't realize is that He was still writing my story.

Questions

1. God created you with a unique identity, that was designed for you alone. What is one trait that makes you special?

2. The experiences we have, and the words spoken over us can damage our God given banners. In what way was your banner damaged?

3. In order to heal, it's important to recognize where your banner is broken. What are some ways your banner is broken?

CHAPTER THREE – THE LIES

The Origin of Lies

John 8:32
Then you will know the truth,
and the truth will set you free.

Knowing how to identify what is true is important for our emotional and spiritual well-being, and is the source of real freedom. But how do we know what truth is?

By the time we are grown up, we've been exposed to both truth *and* lies.

Hopefully as we grow up, we learn to tell the difference between the two. Knowing how to tell them apart is critical, because truth helps us separate what is right from what is wrong.

This can make the difference in how we move forward in life, because getting stuck usually begins with a lie. The Bible says *real* freedom comes when we know the Lord's truth.

John 8:36
So, if the Son sets you free, you will be free indeed.

Everyone I know wants to feel free. The problem is, we often get stuck because what we believe about who we are is not true. Just like the guy at Bethesda, lies can keep us lame, get us stuck, and make us believe we cannot get off our mats.

Lies tell us we are broken, and make us think there is no hope that we can ever be healed. But the truth says, we are loved, healed, and free. It can be difficult to know what to believe. So, how can we tell the difference between a lie and the truth?

First, you have to understand that lies are false statements. Lies are meant to deceive us on purpose. Lies twist the truth and disagree with what God says.

Scripture says, God's words are true.

God's word is truth, and He is truth. It's not what He does, it is the very nature of who He is. And it is because of who He is, that we can be confident what He says is true and reliable.

Here are a few examples of what scripture says:

Psalm 119:160
All your words are true;

all your righteous laws are eternal.

Psalm 119:151
And all Your commandments are truth.

Revelation 22:6
And he said to me, "These words are faithful and true.

John 7:18
Whoever speaks on their own does so to gain personal glory, but he who seeks the glory of the one who sent him is a man of truth; there is nothing false about him.

Titus 1:1-2
Paul, a servant of God and an apostle of Jesus Christ to further the faith of God's elect and their knowledge of the truth that leads to godliness— in the hope of eternal life, which God, who does not lie, promised before the beginning of time,

And there are many more words in scripture that say we can trust His promises are true.

Characteristics of Lies

So, if God is truth, where do lies come from?

Woah, that's a really big question…

If we wanted to pull that question apart, it would take a lot more time, and we'd need to look deeply into scripture. I believe there's a simple explanation. I think we can see the origin of lies, in the third chapter of Genesis.

There's a good chance you've heard this story, but if you haven't let me take you through it.

It takes place in the garden God created for us humans. The garden was more beautiful than we can imagine, and there Adam and his bride, Eve, spent days enjoying everything a perfect world offered.

If you know the story, you may remember the only thing Adam and Eve had on their agenda was to spend peaceful days wandering the garden, naming animals, spending time with God, and enjoying the wonderful place He had created for them.

It was a perfect place. Adam and Eve were never sick, and there was no pain. There was no reason to be sad, no fights or arguments. In fact, there was no difficulty of any kind.

The best part is that, unlike us, they enjoyed a very close relationship with the God of the universe. In the garden, Adam and Eve had a closer-than-your-best-friend-ever relationship with God. It means they experienced Him face-to-face. It's hard to imagine, and fascinating to think about what *that* would be like!

Adam and Eve were free to enjoy everything in the garden. That is, except one thing (Genesis 2:17). The only thing God said they could not do was to eat from one particular tree. From my viewpoint, that one command seems like a pretty small thing, considering everything they *did* have.

Still, even though it might not seem like a big deal, God meant it, and they knew He was serious. God had been very clear about the consequences if they disobeyed. Adam and Eve seemed to understand, and they avoided the tree – for a while.

One day, when Eve was hanging out, the serpent showed up. He slithers up to her and speaks. It's creepy to imagine! I'm not a fan of snakes anyway, and I certainly wouldn't have remained calm if one came up and began chatting with me. But strangely enough, Eve does not seem worried that a snake is talking. She stops what she is doing and has a conversation with him.

It's clear from the story, the serpent is a smooth talker. What he says seems pretty innocent. He's tricky, though. He knows how to control the conversation and he does it without getting Eve nervous.

I often wonder if Eve's internal alarms were going off. You know… the check in your heart that tells you something isn't a safe situation. Whether they did or not, the serpent is clearly leading the conversation where he wants it to go.

He is definitely not just hanging out to chitchat. The serpent knows just what to say to get a reaction from her. Make no mistake, he knows exactly what he's doing when he asks her, "Didn't God say you could eat from ANY tree in the garden?"

It's easy to think the question is innocent, but it's not. It's a question with a purpose. The serpent is asking something that he knows will get a reaction from Eve. He's cleverly trying to get her to doubt what she heard God say.

This was not a new approach for Satan, and it's the same trickery he still uses today. One of the greatest weapons he has is convincing us to doubt God. It's a powerful tool he uses to get us to believe something that is not true. And, once we doubt what God says is true, it's easier to believe more lies.

But Eve doesn't realize this. She continues to engage in casual conversation with the enemy. The conversation seems so harmless, she doesn't even realize she's being set up.

I imagine Eve probably didn't want to be rude, so she continues the conversation. She tells the serpent God said they can eat from any tree except the one. But this is where it gets complicated. Eve enhances what she was actually told. She tells the serpent they are not supposed to eat from the tree "or touch it." Then she adds that if they do, they'll die.

Do you see what happened there? She's starts out telling the truth, but what's interesting is, she adds the part about not touching it. God didn't say that! Ouch. She's added to what God said. She's believing a lie and Satan didn't even have to lift a finger. And, what's really sad is that her statement gives Satan a foothold to close the lid on his deception.

At this point, the serpent is in control. Now, he can run her off the rails, and he does.

He tells Eve a bold-faced lie. He tells her, "You won't die," and then seals the deal by telling her she can be like God if she just takes a bite. Eve is sunk. She bit into satan's lie before she bit into the fruit. She was stuck in her own words.

She couldn't back down, so she took the dare, and tasted the fruit from the forbidden tree. And not only that, she got Adam to try it as well.

Adam and Eve believed a lie and it cost them everything. It seemed so innocent at the beginning. But once doubt came into the picture it ended with the destruction of everything they knew. It changed life for them and for all generations after them.

Common Lies

Adam and Eve's story tells us something important about the power of lies. Their story helps us understand how one little lie sets the stage for the rest of their lives, and for everyone who came after them!

And what's most amazing is this whole situation started with Satan getting them to believe God's promises cannot be trusted.

Lies that cause us to doubt, make it easier for us to believe God cannot be trusted.

Adam and Eve aren't the only ones to believe this lie. I think even today, doubt is the most destructive lies we believe.

One of the biggest faith-struggles we have is believing God's word is true. Just like the guy on the mat who believed he was lame, doubting what the Lord says can keep us stuck.

If Satan can convince us to doubt God's word is true, the battle for our hearts is mostly won. I call this a foundation lie because other lies can be built on it.

Not believing what God says is dangerous. It makes it easier to reject what God promises, what he tells us to do, *and especially* what he says about *us*.

If we think His words aren't true, it's easy to believe lies that say we are not loved and adored by our heavenly creator. And, when we think His words aren't true, it's a lot harder to trust God; never mind believe He's going to heal us.

Psalm 139 says we are fearfully and wonderfully made. The truth is, we are lovingly created by God, with a unique design, and a specific purpose. But it's much more difficult to believe that if we don't trust God's word as the truth.

The good news is, even though Satan would love to keep us trapped as victims; the power of God's words can set us free.

Foundation lies like this can get and keep us stuck.

Beliefs that are the opposite of what God says about us can hold us captive in hurt, and keep us lame. When this happens, it is called a stronghold.

Strongholds often have roots in the words we hear and the experiences we have throughout our lives. I believe figuring out where the lies started is key to healing. The source of lies can be obvious – but not always.

Sometimes, it's difficult to spot where the lie started. However, through the Holy Spirit, with God's help, we can recognize even the most deeply buried lies.

> *2 Corinthians 4:6*
> For God, who said, "Let light shine out of darkness," made his light shine in our hearts to give us the light of the knowledge of God's glory displayed in the face of Christ.

> *John 1:5*
> The light shines in the darkness, and the darkness has not overcome it.

From the moment we are born to the second we die, we interact with the world around us. Everything we hear and go through becomes part of our experience. Some of those things roll off us, but some are absorbed into our minds and hearts.

Our experiences have potential to cast a shadow over us – whether good or bad. That's why the author of Proverbs warns us:

> *Proverbs 4:23* .
> Above all else, guard your heart,
> for everything you do flows from it.

Words are very important. Proverbs 18:21 says words have the power of life or death! And every word either lines up with, or goes against what God says. It if does not line up, it's a lie.

We have to know what's true when it comes to what He says about us. The negative words we hear, or say, have the power to move us towards, or away from God, and what He says about us.

If I asked you to make a list of words to describe you, it's likely you could fill a page. If we're honest, most of us can say a lot about who we are.

Hopefully your list would have a number of encouraging, uplifting, and positive words. What if it doesn't, though? If it's heavy with dark, negative, damaging words, there's a good chance the lies you believe are clouding the truth about who God says you are.

No matter where you come from or where you've been, your past experiences are going to play a part in shaping who you are. In our culture, we are continually blasted by words and pictures that try to tell us who we are, or who we should be. Things like social media, television, books, and music can influence what we believe. The good and bad things we are exposed to blend together and try to tell us what our self-image should be.

Social media has become a huge source of the lies we believe. People we know, and some we don't, use it as a platform to hurt, bully, and destroy. Social media has allowed the bullies of the world to say things they'd never say in person.

Maybe you heard this rhyme as a kid: "Sticks and stones will break my bones but names will never hurt me." It may sound nice, but it's just not true!

Words have a huge role in what we think about ourselves. They are powerful, and usually hurt more than physical wounds.

If you ever doubt it, ask someone who's been bullied.

Lies are damaging no matter where they come from, but when we are close to the one's telling the lies, the damage can be *enormous*. Families should be a place of safety for children, but they are not always. Our families play a big role in who we think we are, and are an important part of our identity.

Not everyone grows up hearing terrible things like I did, but some do. Hopefully, the words you heard told you that you were wanted, loved, accepted, and adored. But, if that's not what you heard, I want you to know this. No matter what was said to you, and no matter who said it, if those words don't align with what God says, they're lies – plain and simple.

Our families aren't the only ones who influence what we believe. *We* also play a part in what we believe about ourselves. When we repeat things we've heard, or add to lies we've heard, it makes the lie more powerful.

I believe everyone has a tendency to say negative things to themselves from time to time. Everyone has done a bit of self-talk. But have you ever said things like this? "Why did you say something that dumb?" "No one cares what you're thinking!" "That was stupid!" "No one likes you!" "You're not good enough."

Remember what I said about lies not lining up with what God says? It's true for our thoughts, too. When we tell ourselves things that are completely opposite of what God says about us, we play a part in damaging our God given identity.

Many times, what we tell ourselves starts from the words we've heard from others. We just add our own twist to the lies and continue telling the lie to ourselves.

Go back and read the story of Eve and the serpent. He gave her the base lie: "Did God really say not to eat from the tree?" Eve's response was to agree and add: "God said not to eat from or touch the tree of life." Remember? God never told her and Adam not to touch it. She was the one who added that.

Here's how it works in the way we talk to ourselves.

Someone says a word like "no," and we change it to "never." We change words like "imperfect" to "damaged." Someone says "dislike," and we hear, "hate." There's an endless list of possibilities, and it often plays a big part in thinking negatively about ourselves.

This was my experience. I certainly heard negative and damaging words. But, even when those voices stopped, I kept the lies alive by repeating them and adding to their power in my life. That's why I want you to recognize what lies are, where they come from, and how they impact your beliefs. If you can understand this concept, it will go a long way in helping you stop the negative self-talk.

We've talked a lot about what lies are. I am guessing some of you are wondering if there's a way you can tell when you're hearing lies. Well, there is. To know a lie, you must first know truth.

I once heard a story about the people who identify counterfeit money. It's interesting because they learn to be experts in what's fake, by studying what's real.

The process is about studying every inch of actual currency. They spend a very long time examining every word, number, image, and line. Once they know what the real deal looks like, they can easily identify what is fake.

It's fascinating, right? It's not possible to know a fake if you don't actually know what is true. This is exactly how we can figure out if what we believe is untrue.

By comparing our beliefs to God's truths, we'll know if we are being told a lie. To know what's true, we have to know what God says.

Let's put it into action, by holding some common, but damaging lies up to God's truth.

Value Lies

One very powerful lie is what I call "The Value Lie."

The Value Lie says you are not worth anything to anyone – especially God! But just look at these Bible verses:

> *Isaiah 49:15*
> Can a mother forget the baby at her breast
> and have no compassion on the child she has borne?
> Though she may forget,
> I will not forget you!

Luke 12:6-7
Are not five sparrows sold for two pennies? Yet not one of them is forgotten by God. Indeed, the very hairs of your head are all numbered. Don't be afraid; you are worth more than many sparrows.

And...

1 John 3:1
See what great love the Father has lavished on us, that we should be called children of God! And that is what we are!

These are just a few scriptures that tell us a lot about our value to God. So, if the lie says we do not matter (especially to God!), when that is held up against what the Bible says, we know it's not true. And it does not matter how we feel.

There are many ways we take this particular lie in. In my case, the words and experiences I had told me I was a mistake. It started the belief that I didn't have value, and all the experiences that came after--sexual, physical, or verbal abuse--just proved the original message was true.

I believed the lie was true because I didn't know what God's word said about me. When I learned the truth, I was able to move past the lie.

Your own lie may have started early, with a powerful experience, or it may have seeped in over time. Can you see a place where this lie crept in? It's great if you do. But even if you don't, you'll recognize the value lie has become truth to you, if you feel invisible, or small. Maybe you think you matter less than others do. Chances are, you've probably even told yourself that no one cares about you.

However the lie slipped in, one thing is true. When someone thinks they have no value, their behavior will always reflect it.

The Value Lie can show up in a lot of behaviors. Just like all lies we believe, there are both acceptable and unacceptable behaviors that can be based on this lie.

Someone who's caught in this lie may constantly look for attention by behaving badly, inappropriately, or in self-destructive ways. It might seem like they have a low self-esteem. They may do things that are self-destructive, or become involved in an abusive relationship.

Sometimes, this lie causes people to believe their value comes from those they hang out with. When that happens, they constantly look to others to make them feel good. This person bases their self-esteem on what others say, or think about them.

Believing this lie can cause us to always agree with whatever the popular opinion is. Often the person caught up in this never has their own opinion, and instead follows along with others, even when they do not agree with their choices.

This lie can be tricky, and it's not always easy to spot.

A person under a Value Lie could be an overachiever, a perfectionist, or the person who excels at sports or in school.

So how do you know if it's the Value Lie keeping you stuck? The biggest clue is what's going on in your head. If you feel like you never measure up to other people, no one cares about you, or like you're invisible, you probably believe this lie.

Look for the words "not," "no," or "never" in your thoughts. Do you tell yourself you are "Not good enough," "No one likes me," or "I'm never going to be happy?" If you use those words a lot, this may be your stronghold.

Look inside and honestly check your heart. The biggest way you'll know this is your stronghold is if you believe you aren't important to anyone – including God.

Grace Lies

Another very damaging lie is the one that says grace is not enough. I call this, "The Grace Lie."

Remember when we talked about the definition of grace? It means getting what we don't deserve.

Scripture says God sent His only son to die for us even while we were still his enemies. In fact, in John 3:16, it says He did that so every one of us could be saved. And in 2 Corinthians chapter five, verse fifteen, it says Jesus died for every one of us.

So, He didn't die for just a few people who have it together. He died for ALL of us. That is grace!

This is really great news, my friends, because God's grace is for you *and* me. And the best part is that scripture says you don't have to earn it. In Ephesians 2:8, we are told it's a free gift to us!

That news should be enough, but the Grace Lie makes us believe we have to work for everything, including God's love. In fact, it makes us believe we have to earn everyone's love. And if we mess up, love will go away.

Many times, people who believe the Grace Lie feel like any time they do something wrong, God will stop loving them. But that is just not true.

Let me be clear. I'm not saying it's okay to sin. I'm saying God doesn't stop loving us when we do. I know this is true, because in Romans 5:8 it says that God sent Jesus to die for our sins while we were still sinning.

You'll also recognize this lie in yourself (or others) if you are always trying to earn love, friendship, respect, acceptance – you name it. The Grace Lie makes us think we have to "do" something to get people to like or love us.

Truthfully, if you need someone to help you out, you probably want to contact the person who believes the Grace Lie. These are the folks that serve at church, help at their schools, volunteer in their community, and run errands for neighbors... And they do those things even when they are overwhelmed or exhausted.

Understand, I'm not saying that serving at church or volunteering is bad. Not everyone who serves is held captive by the Grace Lie. You can tell if they are by looking at what is driving them to serve. Is it their nature to be helpful? Or is it because they feel like they need to earn love or acceptance by doing a lot of stuff?

If you meet someone who is constantly comparing their accomplishments with others, or trying to be like someone they are not, you might be looking at someone who's operating from a belief that there's not enough grace to cover them.

You might even recognize yourself in this.

This lie can be easily missed.

Sometimes it shows up as a strong doubt that we're not doing enough, giving enough, or living up to God's standard. It's not about our call to serve others. And I'm not saying we shouldn't try to obey what God tells us to do.

Someone who believes this lie constantly feels like nothing they do is adequate. They always feel like they aren't "good" enough.

Grace Lies can play out in the person who recommits their life to Christ over and over because they are never quite sure they are saved. Believing this lie can also be what causes someone to run from a relationship with God. Either way, the root is a belief that Jesus's death on the cross was not enough. This person believes that grace is NOT sufficient for us – even though that's what the Bible says.

> *2 Corinthians 12:9*
> But he said to me, "My grace is sufficient for you, for my power is made perfect in weakness."

The Grace Lie can drive us to believe we must earn love - whether God's or others. The truth is, we can NOT earn love from God or anyone! No one can make someone love them.

God's love is a free gift for us.

Grace is getting what we don't deserve, so if you think you need to earn love, forgiveness, healing, freedom, or a relationship with God, you are probably stuck in the Grace Lie.

Hope Lies

The last lie we'll look at is the Hope Lie.

Hope tells us that we can confidently expect there is something good in the future. But this lie says nothing will ever be different. This lie makes people believe there is nothing good for them. One of the worst things about this lie is that it encourages them to give up.

This one's powerful because it not only keeps people stuck, but many times, it stops them from asking for help. Many people, including me, and that guy at the pool of Bethesda, have laid on a mat of hopelessness, year after year because they could not imagine a life that was different than what they were experiencing.

You can see this lie in the person whose life is in a constant mess. They experience trouble every day, and nothing in their lives seems to change.

If this is your lie, you'll recognize it by the feeling that you can't get out of the cycle of bad that you're stuck in.

When someone repeatedly experiences difficult or painful experiences, it can start to seem like they will *always* have difficult or painful experiences.

If someone goes through bad things (abuse, bullying, fear, etc.) over a long period of time, it can cause them to believe things will never change.

Remember how the man laid on his mat year after year when he was only a few feet away from the place he could have been healed? He may have begun to wonder why he should even bother trying to get in the pool.

This lie is one of the reasons we sometimes also continue to stay in our own mess. We remain broken and spiritually, physically, or emotionally lame when the grace and mercy we need is only a few feet away. If you believe the Hope Lie, you'll stay where you are, even when everything points to a way out. And sadly, many times, even when you *can* see a better way, you won't move towards it.

The Hope Lie can keep you stuck, even when the solution to your situation is right in front of you.

I chose to talk about the Value, Grace, and Hope Lies because they are the three core lies that have the potential to keep us stuck. But, in truth, there are as many lies as there are grains of sand.

While I absolutely believe God wants to break down *every* lie, it would be impossible to list every one of them.

My hope here is to expose a few of common ones that I know are at the root of many life problems. These lies are the ones, I believe, most often hold us back, and impact our lives.

Remember our friend at the pool? We can trace the thoughts that held him to that mat back to all three of these lies.

- As a lame man he saw himself as less-than, and believed he had no **value**.
- He did not believe he could receive the gift of healing **grace**, even though he was only a few feet away from it.
- He did not have **hope** enough to grab hold of healing, Jesus offered it to him.

Like him, there was a time that I believed these same lies, and they held me down on my own mat. I believed I had no value, and could never have a different life. I thought there wasn't enough grace to set me free. And I had no hope that my life could be different.

Here's the most important thing you need to know – no matter how big, and how stuck we are because of these lies, we *can* be set free. As powerful as these beliefs are, they *are not* strong enough to stop the healing, redemptive work of God.

I was stuck for so many years. It took a long time for me to get hold of the healing Jesus offered, but you don't have to. We're going to walk this out together. Take a moment now to think about the lies that are keeping you stuck.

Questions

1. Lies that make us doubt God, become the foundation for other lies. What are some of the ways you have doubted what God says about you?

2. Describe some of lies you've heard. How are they different than what God says?

3. What are one or two key lies you've been believing are true?

CHAPTER FOUR – THE STORIES

My Lies, My Truth

Words are powerful. They can bring life to us or they can destroy us. Proverbs 16:24 compares words to a honeycomb that is sweet to the soul and healing to our bones. On the other hand, Proverbs 11:9 says evil words can actually destroy.

No doubt… words are important!

It's not surprising there are so many verses warning us to watch what we say. For example: 1 Peter 3:10 tells us if we love life and want to see good days, we should keep our tongue from evil and our lips from deceitful speech. Ephesians 4:29 says our speech should build others up and should not be offensive. And how about Matthew 15:11? That verse says it's not what goes into our mouth that stains us, it's what comes out of our mouth that does! Yikes!

Whether we understand it or not, words can affect us. The words we hear can shape how we see ourselves, and how we see ourselves can impact our whole life.

When the words we hear are based on falsehoods about who we are, they can change what we believe about ourselves.

When we start to believe what those lies say, they become our story.

The lies that became my own story started before I was born, when my mom decided her life would be better without another child to raise. She felt I was a mistake.

In Psalm 139, it says God knew me before I was created in my mother's womb. So, the fact that my mom considered me a mistake was a lie.

Still, the lie that my life didn't matter began the moment my mom decided to have an abortion. Her decision to get rid of what she thought of as a "problem" told the world – and me – that I was unwanted, unloved, a mistake, and had no value.

It didn't matter that she was stopped before the abortion was completed. By the time I was born, the lie was set in motion. That falsehood became truth to me, and formed the foundation for everything I believed about myself. Every word and experience that came after that event, either agreed with the lie that I was a mistake, or added to it.

Chapter Four – The Stories

The first, and biggest belief that became part of my story was the one that said I should never have been born. The unsuccessful abortion made the lie that I was a mistake seem accurate.

We often believe stories we hear over and over. And that was true for me. Growing up, my mom would often tell me that her life would have been better if I hadn't been born. That gave the lie power, until it became so real to me that I believed it was my story.

The fact that the damaging words came from my mother had a huge impact. For many children, a mother's love is their first understanding of God's love.

It's really not unusual for a kid to believe that what a parent says is the truth. Children are innocent. That's why they believe in Santa and the Tooth Fairy. Make-believe is common for children across most cultures. However, the way kids believe in make-believe, is the same way they usually believe in stories about who they are – even stories that are not true.

That's how it was for me.

Almost every day, my mom told me I was her biggest mistake. She said my birth ruined her life, and she wished I'd never been born. Those are terrible words – no matter who you are.

As an adult, I cannot imagine saying them to a child. But that was my reality growing up and I believed every word she said.

Often when there is abuse, others are not allowed to get too close, so they won't see what's really going on. That is how it was for me. Friends and family were never allowed to get too close. Since we weren't around a lot of other people, there was nothing to compare my life to. There was no opportunity to learn the truth. Without the ability to see healthy relationships, I figured the way we lived was normal, and that what she said must be true.

Like every child, my mom and dad were a huge part of my world. That's how it is for most kids. And even in abusive situations, children usually believe what their parents say.

The things my parents said about me, became part of what I understood about myself. The lie that I was a mistake, became the story I believed. It made me think I did not deserve to be loved. It told me I was responsible for every bad thing that happened in my little world. It made me believe I was the reason my mom was so unhappy and angry. It was the reason she abused me, and why my dad spent so much time away from home.

The story I believed about myself shaped who I became, and influenced the path I took in life.

Everything that happened in my life was filtered through the story that I was a mistake. That belief went so deep for me, it seemed as real as the ground we stand on.

Naming Your Lies

We usually act out what's in our hearts. When we believe lies, they become our truth and go deep into our hearts. And what's in our hearts influences how we behave.

Even scripture says we are shaped by what we believe. In verse seven of the twenty-third chapter of Proverbs, it says that our actions come from our heart.

Here's how that looks…

The lie I believed said I was a was not wanted. That lie became a story that told me I was a mistake. And that story caused me to live like someone who should not have existed.

If we don't want something, it holds little-to-no value for us.

Because I believed I should never have existed, I assumed I did not matter to anyone. This often made me feel invisible.

I always wondered why I was even alive, and because of that, my life didn't seem to matter much. If my birth was a mistake, then I had no value. If I had no value, then why did I exist?

The truth is that on some level, *everyone* wants to matter, and to be recognized. But sometimes people have the core belief that their lives are not important.

When I was little, everything inside me said I did not matter to anyone. The lie also told me that love was never free, and I should not expect it in any relationship. This became a story that told me I did not deserve affection, or attention from anyone around me unless it was earned. And on those rare occasions when I did get attention, I had no idea how to accept it.

The abuse I experienced had shown me there was no need for boundaries. I didn't have a right to say "No," and I certainly had no right to my own body. In my mind, anyone could have full access to me because I believed I had no value. Since I wasn't worth anything, I did not have the right to refuse.

The lie that I was a mistake caused me to become self-destructive. There was no need to be careful since I believed I had no value. My behavior was reckless, and I am convinced that it is only by God's grace that I did not end up in jail, prostitution, or dead.

The abuse I experienced made me hate myself. And that hatred was always lurking beneath the surface, and it constantly threatened to erupt like a volcano.

If I detested myself so deeply, why would anyone else love me? I was absolutely convinced if anyone knew the real me, they'd know right away that I was not good enough. Because I could not love myself, I was depressed, anxious, self-destructive, and suicidal for a good part of my life.

The lie that told me I was a mistake may seem obvious now, but it was very real to me back then.

From the outside, it seems like it should be easy to spot lies like that, but not all lies are obvious. Sometimes you have to look very carefully to find them. And occasionally we need help to see what's not true.

Make no mistake. Even when they are not easy to identify, these kinds of lies are still very damaging, so it's important to try to identify them.

A good way to identify these kinds of lies, is by looking at the behaviors that come from believing them.

For example, one less obvious lie that I thought was truth, was that I would never be good enough the way I was, so I needed to do something to get love.

That belief started because I thought I was a mistake. But it showed up in my life as a need for approval – no matter what the cost. I would do *anything* to get love, approval, and acceptance. Sadly, when we try to make everyone happy, we often end up losing our own identity, and that's exactly what happened to me.

I became a people pleaser at my own expense. In reality, because we're human, most of us have probably done at least a little bit of people-pleasing from time-to-time. But when it drives us to believe we must conform to what other say at any cost, it's a problem. When people pleasing makes anything anyone does to us okay, the result is not going to be good.

For me, this started as a little girl. I remember wanting to please my mother more than anything. Right or wrong, I would do anything to get her approval. In an effort to get her to love me, I became whatever she needed and did whatever I was asked to do to make sure her needs where met.

Even as a very young child, I remember that most of the time, the result was more rejection. Still, I kept trying.

Once in a while, it almost seemed as though my good behavior paid off, and that she was happy with me. There were glimpses of love and kindness from time to time, but the majority of time, my efforts were met with rage and cruelty – not love or approval.

Still, there were rare moments when she seemed less angry. Sometimes she'd bake cookies with me, or patiently teach me to sew. In those moments, I felt like I could barely breathe – I was terrified I'd do something to change her mood again. It made me feel very insecure.

Those times were wonderful, but did not last long. Usually her dark mood would return and she'd spiral into another cycle of verbal and physical abuse. In those times she'd whip me or shove me in our basement.

A favorite punishment of hers was to have me stand against the wall with my arms stretched out in front of me. If I lowered my hands, she'd whip me, so I'd do that for long periods of time – usually until my hands went numb. The punishment was scary and painful. But it never hurt as much as the words she said to me.

Usually, the physical cruelty she dished out, would include verbal abuse so revolting it would make adults cringe. For me, that's when the most damage was done. Words can destroy, and hers left invisible scars that took years to heal.

Still, I loved her. It's a hard concept for some to understand, but children often still love their abuser. I loved her and I wanted her to love me. And, every one-in-a-while, it seemed like what I did made her love me. It didn't *always* work, but it happened enough to convince me to keep trying.

The lesson I learned was that I had to earn love. I thought I could get her to love me by becoming whatever she wanted, or by doing whatever she asked. So, if the path to love was standing behind a chair and brushing her hair until I could barely raise my arms, that's what I'd do. If she wanted me to rub her feet, I did it for hours on end without complaining. I fixed her drinks, brought her food, cleaned up her messes. Nothing was out of bounds if it meant there was a chance, she'd love me.

This need to earn love carried into adulthood. Even as an adult, I did anything I thought would get others to love me.

If the way to friendship or love was to become a doormat, I accepted it. If attention was only gained through sex, I gave in. I believed what I was being asked to do was "love," so I did whatever I had to so that someone would love me.

The most long-lasting lie I accepted as truth was the Lie of Fear.

The Bible says that perfect love (God's love) casts out fear.

1 John 4:18
There is no fear in love. But perfect love drives out fear, because fear has to do with punishment. The opposite is true as well; fear casts out love.

As long as I can remember, my days began with fear. I never knew which mom I'd encounter; the happy mom who baked cookies and sang with me, or the unpredictable, raging dictator mom. I believed I was responsible for her moods, as most kids do. I tried as hard as I could to make sure I didn't make her angry.

Of course, my behavior did not cause her temper to rise. Still, because of her constant blowups, anger, and violence, I felt insecure, anxious, and defenseless. I stopped being a kid, and started being a watchdog. Every contact with my mom involved me trying to decode her mood. I was on guard at all times.

Fear can be draining. At first glance, it may not be easy to see the behaviors that it drives. One common way fearful people struggle is in the area of control. Most of the time, they will try to control anything and everything around them. That's because they believe that if they can control the situation, they won't get hurt.

That's how fear showed up in my own life. It made me try to control everything. Every relationship. Every situation. And every experience.

Like a circus performer spinning plates on poles, I'd run around trying to get everything in my life to stay where I thought it should be. If you've ever witnessed that circus act, you know the outcome is not always good. Sometimes plates fall and break, and that's exactly what happened for me.

The truth is, controlling the word around us is draining, and in the end, usually ends up in a mess.

Fear also made me want to control every relationship I had. For example, if someone I had a relationship with was trying to walk away, I created a situation where they had no choice but to stay. I blocked doors, hid keys, begged – you name it. Instead of that working in my favor, it usually made things worse. It never worked – at least not long term. My desire to control others left behind a trail of shattered relationships.

The more I failed at controlling everyone and everything the more my fear rose. The higher my fear went, the more I tried to control. It became like a terrible merry-go-round that I could not get off. Even though I knew it was not working, in reality, I went around like that for a very, very long time.

Some of the most damaging lies are the ones that go against our understanding of God's relationship with us. For me, the most damaging lie I accepted as truth was the one that taught me love had a high cost. It caused me to believe love was supposed to be dangerous, painful, and must be earned.

What I believed with certainty, was actually a lie that contradicted the truth that God's love for us is pure, and real, and we cannot earn it.

That falsehood took root when, at the tender age of five, I was sexually molested. There are many types of abuse, and each one causes damage in their own unique way. But sexual abuse, often causes deep wounds that are difficult to heal. In fact, sometimes that damage hangs around for a lifetime.

When someone is wounded by sexual abuse, they sometimes confuse the offender's sin with love. Many individuals have struggled to separate the two. That can be a pattern that is hard to change, and the damage it causes can be devastating.

One of the biggest impacts from my own experience was that it caused me to believe sex was a way to get love. In chapter two of Romans, verse 15 says our hearts know the difference between right and wrong. I knew what was happening was wrong, but I also knew it was a way to get love. So, I shoved my natural,

God-given sense of right and wrong as far down as I could, and tried to deal with it.

It was also a powerful lesson that taught me the cost of love sometimes meant doing things that you didn't want to do. It created a damaging view of what love is, made the hole in my heart, and set in motion a terrible belief that ruled my life for years.

The lie that grew out of that experience played out in every relationship I had, especially with men. I thought that having sex was the only way I could be loved, so I gave myself away in hopes that one of them would care for me. I went along with these guys out of fear of rejection.

Here's the thing though, it ended up breaking me even more. The more I gave of myself, the less I felt loved. It became a cycle I repeated far too many times. And every time it tore at me until there was less and less of me.

Not the End

The story of my early life is certainly terrible. It's as hard to tell the story as I'm sure it is to hear it. If the story ended here, it would be tragic. But it doesn't. Just like the man at the pool of Bethesda, I met Jesus and it changed everything.

I promise I'll tell you more about the amazing journey that turned my ashes into beauty, so hang with me.

Right now, were talking about the lies we believe, and recognizing the lies I struggled with, was the way I found healing. I had to figure out what was wrong, before I could understand what was real.

It's going to be the same for you. You've got to start by recognizing the lies. So, what are the lies you've believed?

Once you know what the lie is, you have to compare it with what God says. Remember the story about the counterfeit bill? Just like the fake money, the lie may look real, but when compared with the real deal, it will never measure up.

Counterfeit money cannot be used the way real dollars can. In the same way, a life built on lies can't be used for its intended purpose.

Healing lies begins by trusting God's ability to restore. So, before we start, here's what you need to know…

God prepared a life for you that promises good things.

> *Jeremiah 29:11*
> For I know the plans I have for you," declares the

Lord, "plans to prosper you and not to harm you, plans to give you hope and a future.

His promises are true.

Psalm 119:160
New International Version
All your words are true;
all your righteous laws are eternal.

What God does is always above and beyond what we can imagine or think.

Ephesians 3: 21-22
Now to him who is able to do immeasurably more than all we ask or imagine, according to his power that is at work within us,

These are just a few of many scriptures that show you can trust Him with the process.

Naming Lies

An important step in healing is naming your lies. You do this by taking an honest look at what you believe and compare it with what God says. Remember? Our behavior comes out of what's in our hearts.

Nothing can change until we recognize, and name the lies we believe.

Maybe you recognize some of your own lies through the ones I struggled with. There may be parts of my story that resonate with you, and, if so, you've got a head start on identifying and dealing with the lies in your life.

Still, if you can't see the lies in your own life, that's okay too. I encourage you to take time now to begin to identify them. This is important because the lies you believe are the number one reason you are stuck and just feet from the healing grace and mercy offer.

You need to do this immediately. Remember the man at Bethesda? He stayed stuck, right next to his healing for thirty-eight years! He didn't accept his part in healing – not even when Jesus asked if he wanted to be healed.

It's time, my friend. The choice is yours. You can spend your time desperately trying to find an excuse, so you don't have to participate. Or, you can make today the day you pick up your mat and begin to walk.

Here's what I know for certain: if you wait to name and identify your lies, they will become more deeply rooted in your life and be much harder to move past.

My own healing journey showed me there is power in naming the "bad" thing, because it shatters the secrecy that keeps us stuck.

The lies we believe make up the chains that imprison us. One of the biggest shackles is shame. It often becomes the secret hidden thing we carry around with us. But shame cannot stand up next to God's word.

Psalm 34:5
Those who look to him are radiant;
their faces are never covered with shame.

An important part of identifying your lies, is looking at what you believe about yourself. What are the spoken and unspoken messages you've heard?

This can take some work at first, but don't give up. Remember, lies do not line up with what God says in His word. One of the best places to start counteracting lies is in scripture.

My friends, I get it. Maybe you're saying, "I've tried reading the Bible and I don't understand it." Or, "I don't know where to look." I challenge you to keep trying.

You can also find a Bible translation that's easy to read. Today, more than ever, there are simple ways to access

God's word!

You can find Bible apps for your phone, tablet, or computer. Try doing internet searches like this:

- "What does God say about me?"
- "What are God's promises?"
- *"Scripture that speaks about <<fill in your lie>>"*

As you begin to read what God says about you, think about the words being used. Ask these questions:

- How do the words describe me?
- What do they say about my circumstances?
- What are the promises for my life?

As you dig into what the Bible says, the words will become very healing.

To get you started, here are some examples:

- Believe you're worthless? Luke 12:6-7 says you are worth so much, God numbers every hair on your head.
- Feeling unwanted? Colossians 3: 12 – 13 says you are chosen by God.
- Feeling rejected? Psalm 94:14 says God will never

reject us.

- Without hope? Hebrews 11:1 says that when we have faith it gives us hope – even for things we can't see.

As you begin this process, be aware the most common challenge is confusing what you *feel* with the reality of God's truth.

Decide right now whether or not you believe His word is true. If you believe scripture is true, then it doesn't matter what you (or I) feel. Feelings don't change God's truth.

Ever heard the saying "Fake it 'till you make it?" I encourage you to ignore how it "feels" for now. I promise you, the feelings will come, eventually.

It also matters where you place your focus. Have you ever tried to walk in one direction while looking in another? It's just about impossible. You'll almost always end up where you put your focus. So, concentrate on the one who can heal you.

The Wallenda's are a family of aerialists who, famously, have walked across very high places on very small ropes. It's fascinating and frightening to watch! Years ago, I heard one of them speak about how they manage these amazing feats of balance.

He said, it's all about focus. By concentrating on the end point (the place they are going), they are able to stay balanced.

It works the same way for you and I, friends. Healing can feel a lot like walking a tightrope. You may feel strange at first. It may seem your life is off-kilter. And, there's a good chance you'll have moments that feel like you're going to fall to your death.

But, DO NOT stop.

I encourage you to fix your attention on God and your healing. Don't look around, and certainly do NOT look back where you came from. I warn you; it's going to be tempting because it almost always feels uncomfortable when our lives change.

Take a breath. Trust the journey. And stay focused on learning what God says about you.

Understand, this is a process. You will need to be patient with yourself. The thing with identifying the lies in our lives is that it takes time and it is not always a smooth road. If you get distracted and lose your balance, or fall, get back up. Don't give up. That's the key. One foot in front of the other. One step, then two. Keep moving forward.

Know that the process of restoration is never "done" on this side of heaven. There will always be stuff to address.

Many scriptures speak of us being refined like silver or gold. Take a look:

Isaiah 48:10
See, I have refined you, though not as silver;
I have tested you in the furnace of affliction.

1 Peter 1:7
These have come so that the proven genuineness of
your faith—of greater worth than gold, which perish-
es even though refined by fire—may result in praise,
glory and honor when Jesus Christ is revealed.

Psalm 66:10
For you, God, tested us;
you refined us like silver.

It takes a whole lot of heat to purify silver or gold. But, once
the process is complete, they are beautiful, strong, and resilient.

The process may not always be easy. I don't know about you,
but I find comfort in knowing that it reveals something beautiful at the end.

Friends, please be patient with yourselves. You don't have to
figure this all out today. You only need to begin.

Questions

1. Sometimes words can be more damaging than physical abuse. These words can become lies we believe. What is the most damaging lie you believe?

2. Take a moment and do a search for "What does the Bible say about <your word>"
   - What scripture(s) did you find?
   - What did the scripture(s) say about your word?

3. What is one way you can commit to staying focused on what God says about you?

CHAPTER FIVE – THE HEALING

The Root of Healing

Trees. Puppies. Babies. Love. Faith. Hope. Healing.

Everything begins with a seed, and seeds have the power to birth animals, plants, trees, and human beings.

This is important when it comes to the seeds planted in our lives through experience. Those seeds can set you on a path that will change your life in big ways.

I find it fascinating that even a giant redwood tree begins as a seed. It's amazing to think that those strong and great trees grow to extraordinary heights, are able to weather incredible storms, yet still started as something so small.

I believe nature often gives a glimpse into God's plan for us, and trees are common metaphors in scripture. These Bible stories about trees give us a view into the good, bad, strong, and weak lives of believers.

Just take a look at this verse:

> *Psalm 52: 8*
> But I am like an olive tree
> flourishing in the house of God;

My own experience with scriptures about trees started a long time before I had a relationship with God.

A friend who was a believer prayed Psalm 1:3 over me. That scripture says, "She will be like a tree, planted by the river. She will bear fruit in each season; her leaves will never wither and she will prosper in everything she does."

Wow! Talk about a visual. The tree in this story reflects a life that is whole. The river is a place of safety and nourishment and health.

Since the prayer happened in the thick of my mess, it seemed pretty far-fetched to me. But, little did I know!

At that point in my life, I certainly couldn't see how the words she spoke could ever become a reality. It wasn't until much later that I began to see the beauty in the story of the tree.

What I didn't understand back then was, through that verse, God was promising that (someday) I would be by Him (the river), I was going to be strong, and good things were coming my way.

Even though I couldn't see how that could happen, those words planted a seed. And that seed – although dormant for years – was the beginning of the life I live today.

Friends, my life today is worlds away from the one I lived back then. Let me tell you about my healing journey.

It's a story of how God reached into a pit and saved me from destroying myself. It's where I get to help you see that healing and restoration is not only for me, it's for you, too.

This is where we talk about how the ashes become beautiful.

Healing and restoration in God's hands is an amazing thing. He doesn't just patch the holes; he takes our broken pieces and makes a masterpiece. No detail is spared because he is the master designer. When the process is done God's way, it transforms us to the core. We are rendered new, right down to our roots.

Let me make this clear. It's all about the root.

You see, a healthy tree – and all healthy plants – are fed by healthy root systems. Roots supply nourishment to the tree. If the root is weak or damaged, the tree suffers. However, if the root is healthy, the tree will likely be sturdy. And strong roots that go wide and deep, give the tree stability when the wind and weather push against it.

Just like trees, weeds have roots too. Weeds can be a tiny nuisance that are a blemish in an otherwise pretty garden. But they can also be invasive and a difficult problem that chokes out healthy plants or trees.

There are roots in our lives too. Good and bad things get rooted in our lives. They feed our soul and determine if we are spiritually healthy or not. If left unaddressed, unhealthy, or damaged roots can harm us, or hold us back.

Remember what we said about lies? Lies we believe can take root and cause unhealthy beliefs and behaviors. Traumatic, difficult, or unresolved events like abuse can become so deeply rooted, it can be difficult to remove them.

If a garden is unattended for a long time, weeds can take a lot of work to get rid of. It's just like that in our spiritual lives too. Weeds can overrun and when we first try to remove them, it can seem impossible. In fact, the work may seem so overwhelming, it can be tempting to skip this part of the healing process.

The work of healing requires patience with one's self.

Still, sometimes, change takes work. As you begin the healing process and dig to remove the weeds that have taken over, I encourage you to really commit to the work that it takes.

Understand, I get that it's not easy. I am not a patient person by nature, so I completely get the frustration about the time it takes to clear the way.

It takes a long time to build beauty and strength like the giant redwood trees in Northern California. So, you are going to have to trust God and stay in the process.

It takes faith to believe that God is true to what he promises. He said he'd make me like a tree by the river, and I had to trust that, even though I felt more like a wilted flower in a desert.

Know this, though... His promise was true for me AND it is for you!

Healing takes time, and it's a process. Remember, some of the most magnificent trees take a very long time to grow to their full potential, and so do you!

It's tempting to move forward without going through the process, but I can't stress enough how important it is not to skip out. It's common to feel a little better as you pull up some of the weeds. It's like a pressure valve; letting a little steam out can be a big relief.

But it's only part of the process, and leaving early won't yield the best results.

Some of the lies that have become rooted will be easy to remove. Just like tiny weeds, they are easily plucked out. But there are some that will take a bigger effort to remove. Just like the weeds in a garden, these lies go deep and can take quite a bit of digging to completely remove.

When it comes to those big lies, it's important to remove the whole root. Ever leave part of the root when you pull weeds? Yep... Leaving even a smidge of root will usually result in the weed reappearing. Just like weed-pulling, there are consequences when we don't remove the source (the lie) that's causing us harm.

Remember, the lies we believe drive how we behave.

You'll recognize if a root is still there because it's likely resulting in behaviors, thought patterns, habits, or unhealthy relationships that you just can't seem to get away from.

Listen, don't let the frustration and discouragement cause you to give up. When you start to feel like giving up, recognize the need for help. Go back to the lie. Once you know what it is, you can ask God to help you remove the root of the problem.

The Root of My Healing

I learned about this process as God began to heal my heart.

In the beginning, there were lots of invasive weedy roots to get rid of. I did my best, but to be honest, it was not a pretty process. There were lots of starts and stops and missteps.

For me, the healing process began by tackling one of my biggest lies.

For most of my life, I'd jumped from relationship to relationship, trying to find the one person who'd make me feel loved.

There were different versions of the scenario, but generally the story went something like this: I'd meet a man who seemed to be everything I needed. It usually wasn't based on fact. It was usually based on what I *thought* was truth. Here's what that usually looked like:

New guy: "I'm a nice guy. I have a nice car and a job..." (In truth, he is secretly seeing three other women, has two kids he doesn't support, and does recreational drugs.)

Me: "Okay, that sounds good. I'm in."

New guy: "Can I stay at your place? I'm between jobs." (Actually, he just got fired for stealing from the company, and he can't stay with family because he's stolen from them before.)

Me: (Totally uncomfortable and trying to ignore a gut feeling that I should not let him move in.) "Okay, that sounds great."

These relationships happened way to fast. Most were based on my inner belief that I was unwanted and unloved. I let feelings rule, and never stopped to really look at the situation. I certainly ignored every internal alarm, and pushed aside any boundary or sense of self. I ran full on into bad situations because I believed the only way I could be loved was to give in, even if it meant the results nearly destroyed me.

Not every guy was bad, though. Some were nice, normal, kind guys. The problem in those situations was that I was a mess. I was controlling, or clingy, or sad and distant. It was usually too much for the good ones to handle. Some tried to "fix" me for a while. But it usually didn't take long for them to cut and run. And when they did, it just proved what I already believed about myself.

It's not a big stretch to figure out that my behavior probably had roots in the broken relationship I had with my mother.

Her failed attempt to abort me, the physical, sexual, and verbal abuse, her rejection all drove important messages that became roots in my life. Those beliefs went far down, and it seemed impossible to remove them. In fact, back then, I would have been hard pressed to understand the difference between what she said, and God's truth.

Before you put too much blame on her, I want to point out that she was not alone in the drama, chaos, and abuse. My dad played a part, too. He often worked endless hours to support our family, which can hardly be called "abuse." However, his absence gave my mom free reign to do what she did. He *chose* to be gone even though he knew what she was doing.

More importantly, there were times when he was right there and saw first-hand what she did, but never stopped her. There were times when he'd beat us with a belt just because she told him too. He didn't question her because he was scared of her, just like everyone in the house was.

Still, he was an adult. I learned early on, he was no protector. He was not going to make her stop, or stand up to her when she tormented me or my siblings. And because she controlled him, she kept him from having a relationship with any of his children. His distance left me longing.

As I look back, I realize these were pivotal moments, because they reinforced every lie I believed. Think about it. Kids watch everything parents say and do. With every action, parents are sowing seeds in the lives of their children, and those seeds grow roots.

The seeds my parents sowed were like weeds with roots that grew and tangled. It took years to untangle the root-system of the lies I believed. It was hard work, and some of the roots were painful to remove.

But there is good news.

Even though the root system that had grown throughout my life was complex and deep, healing still happened. Looking back, I can clearly see the point where God began to touch my life long before I knew Him. The healing process began long before even I knew I needed it. And it happened long before I knew where to begin.

My healing started the day my mom died.

It's not what you might think. I didn't find healing because she was no longer around to torment me. It wasn't about closure, because, honestly, I have never put much stock in "closure" when it comes to restoration. It was about God meeting me in the moment my mom passed away. Let me explain.

By the time my parents were in their 70s, I'd moved far away from them. I hadn't talked to either one in about five years when I got the call that my mom had cancer. Our separation couldn't shield me from the sadness and pain that call brought.

I felt like it might be a last chance for us to reconcile. Truly, I knew it was the last chance for everything.

But, there was another emotion. The one that wanted revenge for all she'd done to me. I remember thinking, "Good, she's going to have to stand before God and answer for what she did." As terrible as that sounds, it was real and raw, and it was how I felt.

All those emotions made me feel frozen and unable to decide what to do. Should I go see her or not? In the end, being the people pleaser that I was, I left my home, and my very young son, and went to her side. I hoped we'd have one last conversation where she'd show me the love I so needed from her.

The reality was quite different. There was no last-minute resolution. In fact, even as she lay dying, she said barely two words to me. She mostly ignored me and talked to anyone else in the room. She was rejecting me again. I was crushed.

This was our last chance, and she didn't seem to care.

The day she died, my dad, my sister, and my now adult daughter stood around her. It was surreal. I don't remember crying, but I probably was – we all were. I do remember thinking about how much I wanted her to stand before God and tell Him why she did what she did. I wanted her to suffer like she'd made me suffer. I remember asking God to punish her.

But then her breathing began to slow and I knew her time was getting close. Suddenly something in my heart began to shift. I can't tell you why or how, but I knew in an instant that what she did was because she was damaged. In that moment, I understood that her whole life had been spent wanting love, and yet pushing it away out of her brokenness. I realized how tortured she was.

I knew then that her life had been hell, and that I didn't want God to punish her any more.

Without understanding why, I knew I did not want her to suffer. I said a silent prayer, and asked God to take her in His arms and comfort her. Right after I said that prayer, she slipped away. She died without us ever having the opportunity for closure, but I had experienced a miracle. I had been able to forgive the monster who had tortured me for most of my life.

That was the beginning of my healing.

Understand, though, I wasn't immediately set free from all the trauma and pain. It was years before I truly received healing in any substantial way. Looking back, I am convinced that had I not forgiven her in that moment, my healing would have been delayed or non-existent. I am certain it would not have been as dramatic as it has been.

Forgiveness was the root of my healing, but I am not unique. In fact, it is probably the single most significant part of every healing. I can tell you this, if you refuse to forgive, you're going to limit the work God wants to do in your heart.

Resentment will hold you back and keep the roots of your past firmly planted. I heard it said once that unforgiveness is like drinking poison, and thinking the other person will die. Forgiveness is *not* for the person who wronged you, it's for you.

It's not always easy. It's not usually fun. But it is one hundred percent necessary.

Looking back, I know that God gave me an incredible gift that day. Being able to forgive my mom set me on the road to true healing and freedom.

You need that gift, too.

The Root of Forgiveness

Let's start with the word forgiveness. The word alone can make people feel all kinds of things. But, understanding what God says about forgiveness can be life changing.

It can be defined as a mindful decision to put away feelings of resentment or vengeance toward a person (or group) who has harmed you.

I explain forgiveness as giving over the person who harmed you to God. I picture a meat-hook. You know, the kind butchers use? I imagine taking the person off my hook and putting them on God's.

While we're here, I think it's important to talk about what forgiveness is not. It does not mean the other person was right, or that what they did is okay. It's not justification for the wrong-doer. It doesn't mean the person is not guilty or deserving of punishment for whatever they did. And, it doesn't necessarily mean reunion with the person who hurt you, either.

The most important thing I can say here is that forgiveness does not deny the pain you feel, or the damage that happened to you at someone else's hands. Not at all.

My heart saddens any time I hear it suggested that forgiveness means you need to forget.

You will most likely never forget, but you can, and must forgive. It's God's command for us, and it's the first step in finding freedom and healing. Forgiveness can be a very difficult and painful subject to walk through. That's not lost on me.

Will you stay with me through this subject? You don't have to do anything just yet. I'm only asking that you let what I'm saying sink in before you close the door. As we walk through this, try to keep an open heart and mind.

I understand the story of my mom's death, and my forgiveness of her is pretty dramatic. Most of the time, it doesn't happen that way, and I've never had it happen that way again. But even without God miraculously helping me along, I have to forgive.

It wasn't only my mom. I had to forgive my dad, and the cousin who molested me. And what about the extended family that saw the abuse but didn't intervene? There were many names on my list, and God said to forgive everyone. It was not always easy, but I've had to walk through each one.

In my Christian journey, I've had to forgive not once or twice, but many times since then. Forgiveness didn't end with the people in my family. The truth is, if you are alive there are always going to be reasons to forgive. I've had – and will always have – to obey the command to forgive. God is pretty clear about the need for it.

> *Matthew 6:14-15*
> For if you forgive other people when they sin against you, your heavenly Father will also forgive you. But if you do not forgive others their sins, your Father will not forgive your sins.

Every time I get hurt by someone; I have to face the process of forgiveness. And that's the thing… every time, it's a process.

Understand. This process is so critical to healing. I want to look at steps you can take to move through it, too.

The process of forgiveness can look different for each of us. We all have unique experiences that cause us to need to forgive. Regardless of the reason forgiveness is needed, the steps are pretty much the same.

The best place to begin a journey of forgiveness is by being honest with God.

Remember my angry cry to God to make my mom pay for her sins? I wasn't revealing something unknown, because God already knew my heart; we cannot hide what's going on in there.

It's about being honest with yourself, and letting yourself become completely vulnerable. You need to do that, because you cannot move forward by ignoring what is in your heart.

> *Psalm 139: 24 – 25*
> See if there is any offensive way in me,
> and lead me in the way everlasting.

Try praying like this:

"God, right now, I'm thinking of XX. I'm angry (hurt, sad, bitter… name your emotion) and I want XXX to pay for what he/she did."

The next, step can be challenging, because it's all on you. The only way to forgive is to decide to do it. There's nothing tricky about it. You have to make a choice to forgive the wrong-doer.

You may not "feel" like doing it, but the decision has nothing to do with how you feel. When you choose to forgive, your feelings may not line up with the decision. That's okay.

Make the choice anyway. Remember, it's not about how we feel. It's about what God's word says, and it says we need to forgive.

Here are some ways I've approached it:

- When you first decide to forgive, try praying something like this: "God, I made a decision today to forgive XX."
- After you've made the choice to forgive, you may struggle with the feelings. In those moments, try praying like this: "God, I ask you now to help my feelings line up with my decision."
- When you find the feelings, thoughts, images, or whatever creeping in again, repeat steps one and two.

The last step is to repeat the process as many times, and for as long as you need.

You might get it done with one pass, but it's likely you will need to walk through this process more than once – especially with big hurts and big wrongs. Even with divine inspiration moving me to forgive my mother, I had to choose. And with my father, it took choosing it over and over until one day I didn't need to.

It's not an easy process, but it is an essential one.

We must allow God to remove the deep roots through the process of forgiveness, so he can replace them with a root of healing. The only way through this process, is to walk through it.

From the bottom of my heart, I promise this will work.

God honors our choices to obey. It doesn't matter if the choices we make don't feel good; it still pleases him. And, while we are at it, you don't get extra points if you do it with a good attitude! I know this is true from my own experience, and scripture backs what I've seen in my journey.

Matthew 21: 27 – 31

"There was a man who had two sons. He went to the first and said, 'Son, go and work today in the vineyard.'
"'I will not,' he answered, but later he changed his mind and went.
"Then the father went to the other son and said the same thing. He answered, 'I will, sir,' but he did not go.
"Which of the two did what his father wanted?"
"The first," they answered.

Questions

1. Negative, or bad things can get rooted in our lives. What are some of the roots you've let overtake your heart?

2. Name one root you are willing to let God begin to help you remove.

3. Who is it that you most need to forgive, and how will you start that process?

CHAPTER SIX – THE PROMISES

The Power of Promises

Everyone has made a promise at one time or another. "I promise to take out the garbage." "I promise to keep a secret." "I promise to be true."

Promises can be described as messages that declare who we are, what we will do, or what will happen. They are a pledge, assurance, guarantee, or agreement. Promises can be used to uplift someone or to threaten them. They can offer hope for the future, or certain destruction.

Throughout our lives, promises flow in and over us. They can be spoken or unspoken messages, and have the ability to heal us, or wound us.

We can rely on some promises, but there are others we cannot. The promise of spring after winter is pretty likely to happen. On the other hand, the promise of hope, love, and acceptance may, or may not be a reality in some situations.

The promises we humans make can definitely be unreliable. Promises can be cancelled, forgotten, or changed, and that makes it a lot more difficult for us to believe they are true. And sometimes promises are made with the intention to trick or hurt someone.

Broken, or deceptive promises can cause deep wounds. For those who have been wounded by unkept, or dishonest promises, it can be nearly impossible to trust.

But God is not like us. His promises are reliable.

In the first chapter of James, verse seventeen says there is "no shadow or turning with God." That's big! It means there is no hidden agenda (shadow) in what God says. It means what He says will not change (turning).

Unlike our human declarations and promises, what God proclaims is true and reliable. That's important because, if we're going to believe His promises, we need to know they are true.

The Power of God's Promises

God's promises are different than the ones the world makes. There are over thirty-five hundred promises in the Bible! Everyone is an incredible message of hope. And each one gives us something to cling to no matter what our circumstances are.

God's promises can, and should be, the anchor that holds us steady – especially when the world sends messages that have the potential to topple us.

So why am I telling you this?

I want you to take hold of this concept, because it's the key to overcoming whatever has you captive. God's promises offer hope and healing, but they are of no value if you don't take hold of them.

Remember, it doesn't matter what you feel, because they are true whether you feel it or not. In fact, what God promises for you is true whether you believe them or not!

Here are some examples:

> *Philippians 4:19*
> And my God will meet all your needs according to the riches of his glory in Christ Jesus.

> *James 1:17*
> Every good and perfect gift is from above, coming down from the Father of the heavenly lights, who does not change like shifting shadows.

Isaiah 41:10
So do not fear, for I am with you;
do not be dismayed, for I am your God.
I will strengthen you and help you;
I will uphold you with my righteous right hand.

1 Corinthians 6:11
But you were washed, you were sanctified, you were justified in the name of the Lord Jesus Christ and by the Spirit of our God.

2 Corinthians 5:17
Therefore, if anyone is in Christ, the new creation has come: The old has gone, the new is here!

The foundation you live and operate from must come from what God says, promises, and declares about you! It is a dependable place to build, because His word will never fail.

But anyone who's ever built a house knows the building is only as good as its foundation. That applies here too. If we lay a foundation anywhere else, we will not have a strong place to land when the world around us crumbles.

Just look at these words:

Matthew 7:24-27
Therefore everyone who hears these words of mine
and puts them into practice is like a wise man who
built his house on the rock. The rain came down, the
streams rose, and the winds blew and beat against that
house; yet it did not fall, because it had its foundation
on the rock. But everyone who hears these words of
mine and does not put them into practice is like a
foolish man who built his house on sand. The rain
came down, the streams rose, and the winds blew and
beat against that house, and it fell with a great crash.

If your foundation is fractured, and broken because of past
damage, it will need to be restored as part of your healing journey.

An unhealthy or unstable foundation usually has cracks, and
those empty spaces can be filled with wrong or negative messages. When that happens, it can prevent healing from happening.

Our understanding of who we are must come from a place of
knowing who *God* says we are. When there are holes in what
we believe about ourselves, it leaves room for other people's
words and opinions to filter in. It's nearly impossible to be fully
restored when those cracks are constantly being filled in with
what the world says about us.

As I began my journey of healing, it took me awhile to understand this concept. I would make headway in the healing process only to stumble as soon as the world around me did or said something that reminded me that I was broken. For a while, it felt like I was caught in a cycle of one step forward, two steps back.

It wasn't until I recognized there were large cracks and gaps where wrong messages could still pour in, and make me believe something about myself that was not true. These holes in my foundation allowed the world's promises to fill in the gaps, instead of God's.

A big part of healing and restoration came when I was able to identify where the holes and gaps where. I did that by figuring out where I believed a promise that was not God's. Once I did that, the next step was to fill them with His promises.

That process helped me make permanent changes.

It was pretty easy for me to recognize where the wrong messages from my past had crept in. My mom gave me "promises" such as, "You'll never be wanted," and "You are a mistake." These messages were opposed to God's promises, which say that I am wanted...

1 Peter 2:9
But you are a chosen generation, a royal priesthood,
a holy nation, His own special people, that you may
proclaim the praises of Him who called you out of
darkness into His marvelous light.

And, I am not a mistake...

Isaiah 44:2
This is what the Lord says—
he who made you, who formed you in the womb,
and who will help you:
Do not be afraid, Jacob, my servant,
Jeshurun, whom I have chosen.

Even though my father's messages were unspoken, they were
part of the framework of my foundation. Since he had turned
a blind eye to my mom's abuse, I believed a message that said I
was not worth shielding. That also contradicted God's promise
of protection for me.

Deuteronomy 31:6
Be strong and courageous. Do not be afraid or terrified because of them, for the Lord your God goes with
you; he will never leave you nor forsake you."

Isaiah 41: 10
So do not fear, for I am with you;
do not be dismayed, for I am your God.
I will strengthen you and help you;
I will uphold you with my righteous right hand.

It's not only the promises of our past that affect what we believe later on. Negative or hurtful things we hear and see have a potential to impact us. There's a saying that says, "Garbage in; garbage out." Think about it. If we fill up on a steady diet of unhealthy food, it will likely begin to show up in how our bodies function. I believe that same concept is true in our physical, mental, emotional, and spiritual lives, too.

This is really important because we sometimes add to the garbage, we take in by not being careful about what we let in.

The things we choose to expose ourselves to – for example, what we see and hear – can impact how we think and what we believe. Not sure about that? Binge-listen to only sad, sappy songs, then reflect on how you feel. Some of you won't see a difference, but I bet many of you will.

That's why Proverbs warns us:

Proverbs 4:23
Above all else, guard your heart,
for everything you do flows from it.

We can often control what we're exposed to, such as with social media or television. Those sources of information can have an overload of messages that tell us we do not measure up, aren't good enough, and that others don't like us. My advice? Limit how much time you spend there, or stay away completely. I get that it can be hard to do. But sometimes, it's the best thing you can do for yourself.

When it comes to what others say, we may not have a lot of control over what's said. However, even if we can't control what's out there, we can limit our exposure to what's being said.

What's most important to know, is that no matter what's been said, heard, or seen out there, scripture has the power to change what you've been believing. He can clean out those places that got filled up with what the world says, and replace it all with what *God* says.

You'll recognize wrong messages by looking for phrases like, "I'm hopeless," "I'm not worth anything," "I'm not loved." If a promise starts with "You are NOT," you've probably identified a message that is making your foundation unstable.

The process starts by taking a good look at the foundation of what you believe. Then, identify where the foundation is filled with promises that don't line up with God's. Here's are some questions to ask yourself:

- Whose promises have I been believing?
- What are for the spoken and unspoken messages that may have crept in?
- Where are there gaps or holes caused by believing messages that aren't true?

You don't have to identify every single crack and hole. This is not going to be a once-and-done process. Just begin to look honestly at what you believe.

Once you know where the cracks are, the process to remove and replace goes like this:

1. *Read God's word.*
2. *Ask God to remove what is not aligned with His word.*
3. *Read His word.*
4. *Repeat steps 1 – 3.*

The Power You Need

The Word of God is the most powerful tool we have when it comes to breaking down lies and strongholds. God's word is different than any other written text, because it tells us His truth, His promises, and what He believes about us!

You won't find a better path to restoration and wholeness. Although there are some great self-help books and programs out there, there is power in God's promises because *His* words are true.

Remember, there is no shadow or shifting with God!

One more thing. I pray you come to know and trust God's word. But even if you don't, the process still works if you don't believe His promises for you. That's the amazing and miraculous way God's words work.

Look at this scripture:

> *Isaiah 55:11*
> So is my word that goes out from my mouth:
> It will not return to me empty,
> but will accomplish what I desire
> and achieve the purpose for which I sent it.

It means that no matter what, God's words will always accomplish their intended job.

So, what if you have no idea where to start? Well, there are several ways to find verses. You could pick up a Bible and search for scriptures. I'm going to be labeled a rebel for this, but I believe that method is the least effective when you first start doing this.

I recommend you either find a good Bible App for your cell phone, computer, or tablet. Many of them have a feature that lets you search by specific words, such as hope, love, fear, or others. A digital Bible may have options to search, which would be helpful. And, there are print or digital books that list God's promises. Any of these options will get you started.

As for where to start, I suggest you to look for promises that resonate with you. Once you find them, hold onto them so you can refer to them often.

You can do that by writing them on your bathroom mirror, or put them on sticky notes on your desk or in your car. Add them to the home screen of your cell phone. Write them in a journal or notebook. Keep them in your wallet or purse.

Do whatever it takes to make sure they are in front of you often. These words will become your lifeline as you begin to grow and heal.

There are so many things we hold on to. Some are good, but some are not. God's word is something that can transform your life, so why not take time to dig in?

The biggest changes in my life have come through God's word. It's helped me grow, it's challenged me, comforted me, inspired me, and directed me.

In short, reading and exploring scripture is the best thing you can do, if you want your life to change.

Let me get you started. On the next page is a list with just a few of God's promises.

I've included some of the common things we think or say, what God says about those statements, and the scripture verse that applies to the topic, so you can check it out yourself.

Take some time now to read through them.

YOU SAY	GOD SAYS	BIBLE VERSE(S)
"It's impossible."	All things are possible through me.	Luke 18:27
"I'm too tired."	I will give you rest.	Matthew 11:28-30
"Nobody really loves me."	I love you!	John 3:16 John 3:34
"I can't go on."	My grace is sufficient.	II Corinthians 12:9 Psalm 91:15
"I can't figure things out."	I will direct your steps.	Proverbs 3:5-6

YOU SAY	GOD SAYS	BIBLE VERSE(S)
"I can't do it."	You can do all things through me.	Philippians 4:13
"I'm not able."	I am able.	II Corinthians 9:8
"It's not worth it."	It will be worth it.	Roman 8:28
myself."	I forgive you!	I John 1:9 & Romans 8:1
"I feel all alone."	I will never leave you.	Hebrews 13:5
"I'm afraid."	I have not given you a spirit of fear.	II Timothy 1:7
"I'm worried and anxious!"	Cast all your cares on *Me!*	I Peter 5:7
"I'm not smart enough."	I give you wisdom.	I Corinthians 1:30

Let me give you one more bit of advice. Be consistent. Nobody gets into shape by visiting the gym once in a while. It takes commitment.

It's important to flood your mind with what God says.

When you continually read His promises, you will notice the words begin to shape what you believe. This is what it means by "transforming your mind."

Romans 12:2
Do not conform to the pattern of this world, but be transformed by the renewing of your mind. Then you will be able to test and approve what God's will is—his good, pleasing, and perfect will.

The more you read scripture, the easier it is to begin believing the promises are true for you. And the best part of this, is that the longer you hold onto his promises, the fewer gaps there will be to fill with the wrong stuff.

If you want to know when to start, the answer is now. Why wait to begin a journey towards wholeness and healing? Remember our friend at the Pool of Bethesda? Jesus didn't tell him to pray on it, ask his friends for advice, or wait for a sign. He told the man to stand up. This means the man had a role in his healing. He had to move into it for it to start.

Step into Your Sea

If you really want to find healing, you're going to have to be part of the solution.

Think about the Bible story in Exodus chapter fourteen, where Moses is leading the Israelites out of Egypt. Maybe you know that story, but if you don't let me tell you about it.

In the story, Moses and the Israelites are being chased by their former captors. It's a dramatic scene, and as they try to outrun the Egyptians, they find themselves at the banks of the Red Sea. Talk about being between a rock and a hard place. At this point, their choice is to drown in the sea, or be killed by the Egyptians.

They believe they're certain to be captured, and probably killed unless God intervenes… and intervene he does! Moses prays for God's help, and what does God do? He instructs Moses to tell them to move forward first. Once they stepped towards the sea, THEN God has Moses raise his staff to part the sea."

Wow, they played a part in this miracle. The moment they take that step into it, God does a miracle and they are able to escape to freedom.

This is important stuff, my friends!

God had them STEP forward towards the sea before it parted. There was no laying on the sidelines waiting until the way through was created. They had to walk forward, and trust God.

And guess what? It's like that for us, too. We cannot wait for someone else to do this for us. It doesn't work if we just lay down and hope for things do be different.

Nope. We have to take a step towards it.

So, what is your sea? What challenges are keeping you from stepping forward? Maybe you're like the man at the pool. Maybe you've laid on that mat for so long believing you are "lameness," that you don't even know how to move. Or, it could be that you're like the Children of Israel, and you're being chased by the past. What is making you believe that you are paralyzed at the edge of your healing? You need to identify and call out whatever is causing you to hesitate right now.

When will you step into your sea?

The process may look slightly different from one person to another, but in almost every case, it begins the same way. Look at the man at the pool and the Israelites. In both stories, the answer was to just do it.

Want another example? Look at chapter six of Joshua. In order for Joshua and the children of Israel to topple the walls of Jericho, and take hold of the land God had promised, they had to march around the city for six days. Then, on the seventh day, they had to march around it and blow trumpets. I bet it seemed pretty strange at the time, but they were obedient and it worked; the walls fell and they were victorious.

These are great examples to show us that we just need to take a first step. The moral of the story is this. Sometimes it will feel strange, but you still need to do it.

The good news is that once we do, God will always show up – just as He promises. Need a reminder of some of God's promises? Well, for starters:

- He promises a future and a hope. (Jeremiah 29:11)
- He promises to restore us. (Ruth 4:15)
- He promises we will find joy. (Psalm 51:12)
- He promises to restore the wasted years (Joel 2:25)
- He promises to heal your damaged soul. (Psalm 23:1- 3)

Take hold of his promises for you. They are true. They are powerful. They are trustworthy. And they are yours.

Questions

1. In what ways are the promises we make to each other different from the promises God makes to us?

2. Thinking about some of the promises that God give us, which one is the hardest to believe and why?

   Which one is easiest to believe?

3. Just like the Israelites, we usually have to step towards what God's doing in our lives, as an act of faith.

   Why (or why isn't) the thought of moving forward difficult for you?

   How can you break through that challenge?

CHAPTER SEVEN – THE PEOPLE

Don't Travel Alone

One of the most powerful forces in the healing journey are relationships.

As humans, we share a need for belonging. In community, we find a common thread with others. In healthy relationships, we help, comfort, and support each other as we move through life.

Every season of life is better when we have relationships with others.

Scripture has many examples of the power of friendship, so it's clear that God created us to be with others. Look what it says in Genesis:

> *Genesis 2:18*
> The Lord God said, "It is not good
> for the man to be alone.

We need people in good times, and we need them in the hard times, too. This is especially true when we are walking through seasons of healing. Restoration and healing are not easy, and isolation will stop or hinder the process.

We need each other, especially when we are walking through challenging times. You're going to need others around you to hold you up.

Trying to do this alone is like climbing Mount Everest without guides. Sure, there's a small chance someone trying to make that climb could make it on their own, but the majority of people that make the difficult journey are in groups. That's especially true for anyone who's not made the climb before.

I love the story of Moses and Aaron in verses ten through thirteen of Exodus chapter seventeen. It's a great example of how community can help us through the hard stuff.

In this story, Moses, Aaron, and Hur are on a hill watching Joshua fight a brutal battle below. As they watch, Moses holds his staff up and Joshua wins. If he puts his arms down, Joshua loses. Well, this works great until Moses' arms get tired and he can no longer hold them up. It could have meant defeat, but his friends did not let him down. Aaron got on one side and Hur on the other, and they held Moses arms up.

To be clear, you are not stronger than Moses. None of us are. We need people around to hold us up when we get tired, discouraged, or when we lose hope.

The right relationships can mean the difference between winning or losing the healing battle. When we don't have the strength to keep going, friends can keep us from giving up and help us find ways to move forward.

We need people to encourage us. That's what this scripture says.

Galatians 6:2
Carry each other's burdens, and in this way you will fulfill the law of Christ.

A circle of the right people can aid in healing by helping to removing roadblocks, especially the ones you, yourself put in place. There are times in the healing process that you may need a gentle (or sometimes more forceful) nudge to help you move away from thinking and behaviors that are holding you back.

Good friends can often see you are about to fall off the road long before you do. When you are on a difficult journey, it's always good to have people to warn you of danger up ahead.

The biggest reason you need to have the right people in your life is because we are better in groups. Look at this scripture:

Ecclesiastes 4:9-12
Two are better than one,
because they have a good return for their labor:
If either of them falls down,
one can help the other up.
But pity anyone who falls
and has no one to help them up.
Also, if two lie down together, they will keep warm.
But how can one keep warm alone?
Though one may be overpowered,
two can defend themselves.

This verse is often read at weddings, but it's not only about husbands and wives. It's about how we support each other – all of us in community. Together we can get more done.

Walking the road to healing by yourself is going to take longer because you need others to push you onward. In many situations in our lives, we need others to motivate us to keep going. Have you ever seen the crowd that gathers along the route of a marathon? They may be there because they love the sport, but I will venture to guess a fair share of them are there to cheer someone on. We all need cheerleaders as we move along our own healing path.

A journey of healing and restoration is rarely done without at least a few ups and downs. When you are sitting on the floor in a heap of tears trying to remember how or why you started this journey, you need others to help set you on your feet again.

When we fall down, the people around us can help us to get back up. We can stay stuck in misery a long time when there's no one to pull us back up.

My advice is to find people to support you. You don't want to walk this process alone. This was a critical part of my own healing journey. There is strength in community, and it matters who you have encircling you on this journey.

Forms of Community

Let me be totally clear about this. Not everyone you know should be part of this circle.

I can tell you from my own experience, the people I surrounded myself with were especially important in my healing process. But not everyone I knew was part of that group.

This can be a tricky process. Since part of your healing involves making good choices and having good boundaries, you are going to have to choose your circle carefully. I'm not encouraging you to judge people, but I'm recommending that you be aware that some people will help you in the process; some will not.

Here are some questions to ask yourself to determine if you are with people who will help your healing:

Are the people you hang around part of the problem, or part of the solution?

You don't want the people who ran with you on the old path to be the ones walking you out of it. Look at this scripture:

> *1 Corinthians 15:33*
> Do not be misled: "Bad company
> corrupts good character.

Will they help you find out what God says rather than giving you solutions that the world offers?

Look what the author or Proverbs says:

> *Proverbs 13:20*
> Walk with the wise and become wise,
> for a companion of fools suffers harm.

Have they walked a journey of healing, or are they stuck themselves?

People who've been through what you're going through under-stand the journey.

> *2 Corinthians 1:3-4*
> Praise be to the God and Father of our Lord Jesus Christ, the Father of compassion and the God of all comfort, who comforts us in all our troubles, so that we can comfort those in any trouble with the comfort we ourselves receive from God.

When trying to figure out who should be walking along side you, it can be very helpful to start by first looking at the people you should consider eliminating from your life. Do not include people who…

Feed into your misery.

I believe the saying "misery loves company" is absolutely true. Proverbs 12:26 says good people guide their friends, but the wicked lead them off course.

When we're broken, we often like to hang out in our pain, especially if there are others there to feed into it. Resist the urge to find other people who play into your situation and keep you feeling like a victim.

Enable you.

The worst thing that can happen to you on this journey, is having someone who helps you stay stuck on your mat.

You need people who are good enough friends to speak truth, and challenge you when you are falling back into old habits. 1 Thessalonians 5:14 instructs us to encourage those that feel weary and weak.

Tear you down.

Avoid people who make you feel shameful, broken, or small.

The truth is you do not need those people in your life ever. But, be especially careful to stay away from people that put you down during the healing process.

If someone is tearing you down, you need to separate from them physically or emotionally! Allowing yourself to be around people who tear you down, will continue to feed you the lies you are trying to escape.

Encourage you to remain a victim.

Oh my, this one is so important! You will never fully heal if you keep identifying yourself as a victim!

Many times, the people who do this are coming from a place of caring. They care about you, and feel bad for you, so they try to help.

Make no mistake though, this is NOT healthy for you or them. This is a relationship that will also keep you stuck in your pain. Look again at how Jesus spoke to our friend at the pool.

> *John 5:6*
> When Jesus saw him and knew he had been ill
> for a long time, he asked him, "Would you like to
> get well?"

Notice he didn't sympathize, or let the man remain a victim. He simply asked the question.

The people around you are going to have the opportunity to speak into your life. So, as you form your circle, there's one person you're going to need to keep in check. The biggest troublemaker is going to be the old voice inside you! That voice is going to be the one that tries to get you to believe the same old lies, and to make the same old decisions.

Just in case I'm not being clear, this is you, my friend. I'm talking about the person you see in the mirror, and who follows you around all day.

Break up with her.

I'm not kidding. You have to make a mindful effort to remove that old voice. And I'm telling you, she usually won't leave without a fight.

Breaking up with the old-you is going to be one of the most important things you'll do! Old-you is going to try to follow you around and get you to listen. Take my advice. Any time you hear that, do what you need to do to get rid of it!

If you aren't sure what to do, here's a few suggestions:

- Keep one of the scriptures you identified in the last chapter near you. When the old voice gets loud, use the verse you wrote down to silence her. *Tip: Say it out loud!*
- Keep an inspiring, empowering song nearby. When the inner you rises up, play that song on full volume. *Tip: I highly recommend singing along loudly.*
- Talk to the people in your circle and ask them for help. That's what they are there for. *Tip: Create a group text so you can let them know when you need help and prayer.*

The question now is this: "How do you know who to choose for your circle?"

Finding the right people is important, and choosing the right people can be difficult. But with thought, prayer, and honesty, I'm confident you can find the right people.

So where should you look?

For starters, there's a good chance you won't find them in the people you are the closest to. That's especially true if they've been your friend for a really long time. You may also want to avoid people that are part of your family.

Here's why.

Family and close, longtime friends usually have an overly soft spot for you. That means they may not be able to provide balanced guidance or support. Sometimes those people love you too much to be objective.

So, who do you choose? Here are some of the people you should consider bringing into your life.

People who challenge you.

The people in your circle should be willing to challenge unhealthy or "backwards" thinking. You may not like this, but having someone come along to your pity-party is not going to help you move forward.

Beautiful Ashes – Student Edition

People who speak truth to you.

You need honesty and truth, but not just any truth. The best people are going bring you back to God's truth. I'm not implying you need to hang around people who can quote scripture by chapter and verse. The exact location of the words is less critical than the reminder to you of what God says, especially now.

People who make you own your actions.

Oh my, this one is SO important. This was one that I liked the least, but it was also the one I needed the most. What that did for me was help me realize that I owned the consequences of the choices I made – good or bad. It's time to own up, sisters. Remember, you don't have to like it; you just need to have it.

People who sharpen you.

Look for people who are willing to be the kinds of friends who will push you forward. In order to grow, you need to mature in your understanding of who God is, and what His word says.

People who are willing to disciple you are important to have along in this process.

Now that you know the *types* of people who should make up

your circle, where are you going to find them? Let's look at some of the options.

Let's start with the community that's probably most readily available – the local church. There is so much to be gained by connecting with others within a church. Churches and youth groups are available almost anywhere. If you are already attending a church, or even if you occasionally attend a church, you are halfway there.

If you don't, I will suggest that you ask people you trust where to find a good, Bible teaching church.

Churches and youth groups can provide a sense of belonging, and can provide the support you need on this journey. Belonging to a church is a great way to meet like-minded people.

I wish I could tell you it's always safe at church, but, unfortunately, I cannot. Most of the time, they are filled with well-intended people, who are seeking a relationship with God, just like you. But you do need to watch out for a few things.

Churches by nature attract messy people. That's okay. Just be mindful about having people who may be struggling, just like you, trying to pour into your life.

The biggest thing to watch out for are people who will pull

you back. Go back and read the section about who not to invite into your circle. That should sum up what to look for.

A great place to walk through healing is in a small group. If you're female, and working through stuff, I suggest groups that are all female. First, other women (young or old) will understand you in a way the opposite sex cannot. It's not a slam on males, it's just a fact that we are wired differently and, therefore, do not process things the same way.

A small group will provide a safe place where you can walk through your healing. If you can find a group of young women who have already walked the path you are on, even better. And if the study is about healing from your past, you've probably got a winner.

The fact is, whether we're young or old, we need a community of women. If you haven't experienced the amazing healing and restorative power of girlfriends, I encourage you to try it. For me, girlfriends have been the salt and light I needed – and still need – to stay on course in my own life journey.

Finding small groups is not super hard. I recommend you start at church or ask friends. As for what to look out for, I again point you to the section about good and bad circles!

Another kind of community can be found with one-on-

one mentors. There are lots of fancy definitions for mentors, but for this purpose, I'm talking about someone who teaches, advises, or guides. You need this kind of support because a good mentor is able to provide you with real, honest, unbiased advice.

The best mentors have experience in the kind of healing journey you are walking. An experienced mentor will be able to help by providing the kind of perspective someone without that inside view may not have. They will probably understand the pitfalls and traps you could encounter on the road to healing.

From a practical place, they can help you look at situations objectively, and identify steps that will get you where you want to go. They are helpful when you are confused or have decisions to make, and they provide encouragement on the way.

Since a mentor should be a trusted person in your life, you'll want to choose wisely. There are two kinds of mentors: those who volunteer, and the ones you hire. There are good and bad sides to both options.

Either way, you don't want someone that is going to lead you off track or give you advice or suggestions that go against what you're trying to accomplish.

Mentors can be found at churches and community service

groups, or through local counseling agencies. But you'll probably want to work with your parents, guardians, or youth leader to find a mentor.

The journey you are on will not always be easy, but it will be lighter with support. Take time now to identify your circle of support.

Chapter Seven – The People

Questions

1. Why is it important to have people around who can walk the journey of healing with you?

2. Who do you need to step away from? Who are the people you need to have around you?

3. Why should you avoid people who tear you down, help you remain a victim, or encourage you to stay unhappy? How can they hold you back?

4. Name one person you are going include in your circle.

CHAPTER EIGHT – THE BEAUTY

Ashes and Beauty

Ashes are what's leftover when we burn something. Think of a firepit the day after.

We don't usually place value on the leftover ashes. Most of the time we just throw them away. We certainly don't admire them, we don't call them beautiful, and they are not usually put on display!

That's how it is with the hard things that happen in our lives. Often, we consider the difficult things in our life as a waste. Sometimes we push the memory of them away from us. But too often, we hold them up high like some kind of trophy that tells everyone how hard our lives have been. Think of it a bit like comparing scars.

My life verse – the one I cling to, and live by is Isaiah 61:3. In that verse it says that God will give you beauty for ashes you've had in your life.

My past certainly had its share of ashes, and I love that the verse says he can take those broken things in our past and make them something beautiful. That's the story of where I came from and where I am today.

Maybe the part about the ashes makes complete sense. But I bet some of you are wondering what exactly the scripture is talking about when it refers to "beauty." I'm guessing for some of you it's not a word you can relate to.

Let's look at that.

Most of the time, the word "beauty" is used to describe physical beauty. But it can be used to define nature, experiences, music, art, places, and even cars. In our culture you might say it's even an often-overused term.

Plus, the concept of beauty is subjective – that means there are many different definitions of beauty. That's why you may have heard it said, "Beauty is in the eye of the beholder."

What exactly does it mean then, when scripture says God will give us beauty? Well, put simply, we could say that beauty is a combination of qualities or abilities.

That definition is okay, but it seems again to point to the physical aspects of beauty. To me, it's so much more.

I describe beauty as every good thing. That means it relates to everything we can see, hear, touch, taste, or feel. Beauty is around us and through us. It has shape and color and texture and smell. It's whatever is true and noble and lovely and admirable.

I believe this kind of beauty describes the best of what God creates.

Now I want to stop you before you get side tracked, and start relating this to how you feel about your own looks. This is *not* about how we look. The Bible clearly says beauty is not about the external. It's about what's inside. Look what it says in 1 Peter:

> *1 Peter 3:3-4*
> Your beauty should not come from outward adornment, such as elaborate hairstyles and the wearing of gold jewelry or fine clothes. Rather, it should be that of your inner self, the unfading beauty of a gentle and quiet spirit, which is of great worth in God's sight.

From God's perspective, you *are* beautiful. In fact, in the Song of Solomon, He says just that!

> *Song of Solomon 4:7*
> You are altogether beautiful, my darling;
> there is no flaw in you.

That's right friends, God, the creator of the universe, the one who created the stars, flowers, sunsets, and every amazing thing you can imagine has declared that you are beautiful! And you don't have to feel it or believe it for it to be true. It just is.

The beauty being spoken of in Isaiah 61, goes much deeper than what's on the outside. What I learned through my journey is that what God is talking about here, is the restoration of the identify he created for us before we were born.

That's huge, my friends, because with God's brand of beauty, you are free to be the person you were always meant to be. Think about the things you secretly wanted to do. Think about the talents and skills you have that you're too afraid to share with others. Think about the things you want to do in your life that feel like they could never happen.

God's beauty is all that and more.

Still, let me be clear. God's version of beauty does not include some secret potion, success driven, Santa-in-the-sky life.

Life doesn't just go away with healing. And as long as "life" exists, there is going to be difficulty and sadness from time to time. There will always be hard stuff in our lives. There's no person that ever lived who didn't have some ashes in the story of their life. Ashes are what's left over when everything is burned away. It's what remains after suffering, heartache, hurt, abuse, or tragedy.

The hard stuff we experience (the "ashes") can be used by God to grow us, bless us, and to eventually encourage others who may be going through their own seasons of trouble.

God's promise is one of hope, birthed from the ashes. The power in Isaiah 61:3 is in the declaration that God can take the burned-up mess of our lives, and, out of it, create something of beauty.

I am always in awe of the way God creates beauty out of the trials and troubles of today, yesterday, and tomorrow. The best part of this is that He doesn't just promise to patch up the holes in our banners, and send us on our way. No, God's work is one of complete restoration!

In the process of restoration, He is making us beautiful works of art. He is a master artist, and through His hands, our pain becomes magnificently beautiful.

I know this to be true for me, and I want you to know it is true for you, too. This is a promise of hope.

Don't let yourself fight this concept just yet. I absolutely believe there is a spark in there just waiting to be fanned into a glorious fire where God's light shines through you.

Do something for me, please. I want you to take a moment now. Close your eyes. Take a deep breath and look. Do you see it? Look for that little light deep down. I promise you, it's there.

With everything inside me, I believe that beauty can come from the ashes in your life. Look at these promises of restoration:

> *Isaiah 61:7*
> Instead of your shame
> you will receive a double portion,
> and instead of disgrace
> you will rejoice in your inheritance.

> *Psalm 103:2-4*
> Praise the Lord, my soul,
> and forget not all his benefits—
> who forgives all your sins
> and heals all your diseases,
> who redeems your life from the pit
> and crowns you with love and compassion,

Restoration happens as you let God in and allow Him to heal you.

Don't have ask if it's possible; it is.

Don't have to ask if He can; He will.

Chapter Eight – The Beauty

The Lord sees you and loves you. He created the universe, He planned you, and He wants you to be whole.

I tell you this with love and honesty because I know it with my entire being. It's the journey I've walked, and the reason I write.

For me the journey from ashes to beauty took time. It was not overnight, but as my healing took root, I began to see the shine underneath the wreckage. Today, as I look back, I can clearly see all the ways He created my beautiful ashes.

Let me give you a glimpse into God's amazing handywork.

Despite the pile of broken relationships in my past, I can say that today, I'm happily married to a man who understands and loves me for who I am. But God didn't just send a guy my way. Nope, He created a story, I could never have imagined.

It's actually a bit amusing how it all played out. You see, I met my hubby online. Now, hear me out. This was pretty funny because I had given every one of my friends who tried online dating a hard time. I used to say, "I can meet crazy people in person, I don't need to meet them on the internet!"

Well, if you don't think God has a sense of humor, get this. I met him because both he and I were stalking our high schoolers' social media accounts. Our boys went to school together, and he found my account through his son's.

When he reached out to me to say, "Nice smile." I was tempted to delete it. But I read his profile and it was all about the importance of forgiveness. I was intrigued. But it wasn't until my son said "Hey, I know that guy's son." That I sent my one-word response, "Thanks."

For the next few months, we went back and forth. The messages were not very person – mostly small talk. But they gave me an idea who this guy was. Eventually, he asked me on a first date, so we met for lunch. That first date ended up being three hours long, and we started dating shortly after. But God wasn't done yet.

After a month or so of dating, I was praying about how to bring up the subject of sex before marriage. See, I wanted to follow what I believe is "God's" plan, and wait until marriage. But how was I going to bring that up? At that point we hadn't even kissed!

Well, no problem for God. Right about that time, he came to my church for the first time. Want to take a guess what the sermon was about? Yep, sex before marriage. Later, I asked what he thought. (I didn't want to give away my opinion just yet!) He said something to the effect of, "What the pastor said was true. I don't think we should have sex if we aren't married."

What? God knows better than we do what needs to be said, how it should be said, and when!

We were engaged six months later, and married six months after that. And on our wedding day, as I walked down the aisle, I saw the man God brought me, who loved me enough to wait. It was one of the single most powerful ways God healed my heart because for the first time ever, a man loved me for who I am, and not for what I gave.

One of my favorite memories from our wedding day, was walking down the aisle. We were married in a tiny little chapel. The sun was setting over the lake and you could see it behind the altar. Our closest family and friends had all gathered to celebrate with us. It was picture perfect! And when I got to my handsome groom waiting for me, he whispered these words, "Do you see him?"

See who? I must have looked puzzled because he motioned behind him and there in all his glory was 1970's Elvis! Well, not the real one, but a darn good impersonator! It was funny and beautifully thoughtful at the same time!

Let me explain why.

About one month into dating, he asked me to marry him. He says now he knew on our first date, but I wasn't even close to that place when he said it out loud. So, to avoid the situation, I decided to be silly. I told him I'd only marry him if Elvis could marry us!

Well, as months went on, he asked a few more times, and the answer was always the same. So, since our pastor refused to dress up as Elvis for the wedding, my loving groom found an Elvis to be part of the ceremony. Seriously, can you imagine?

I could not have invented or imagined this man. He was not my usual type. But the man God provided was everything I didn't know I needed. He makes me laugh, and loves the crazy, silly, messy girl that I am.

Because he appreciates and loves the personality God created me with, I have permission and empowerment to be who I truly am. He loves the hippie in me who likes funky music and clothing styles. He encourages me to be the artist and writer that God created all those years ago. And the funny, snarky, passionate lady inside, is the one he lets bloom.

Laying on my bed as a little girl, beaten and battered, I could not imagine a life filled with family and friends. All I could see was the pain and ugliness the world provided.

That awful view of life captured me, and held me for many years.

It nearly caused me to give up. But praise God, I didn't.

I was broken and lame for years, until I had to face the same question Jesus posed to the man at the pool, "Do you want to be healed?"

For me, that moment came after I experienced the heartache of being dumped a few weeks before I was supposed to wed a man I barely knew. Looking back, I was headed straight towards another messy ending.

Today, I can see it would have ended in disaster, but back then, I desperately wanted it. In my brokenness, I thought that relationship would bring me happiness and I'd finally be loved. When it ended, I was devastated. I came close to giving up.

But, being shattered and brokenhearted was what finally got me to look towards God and His promises.

Ever heard someone say, "Sometimes the worst thing, is the best thing that could happen?" Well, that's how it was for me. I didn't know where to go, and I wasn't sure what to do. But, in that moment, I made the decision to get up from my mat. That's when I chose to stand.

I have to imagine our friend on the mat was scared and weak as he took those first few steps. That's how I felt, anyway. I'd experienced God in my life from time to time before that moment, but I always stayed right there on my mat. God had begun to touch my heart years before I knew it. I'd heard people talk about how He healed them, but it wasn't until I got up and took a step that I began to truly heal.

Moving Forward

Healing is not easy, and it takes time.

As I moved through each part of my healing, I learned to give myself grace, and embrace the process.

There were times along the way, when it seemed I made progress. And there were times when it felt like I didn't move at all. Sometimes it was painful. Sometimes it was hard. But the reason it worked is because I did not stop.

When I got tired and wanted to give up or sit back down, I called my circle to help me get moving again. If I fell, I got up. If I got lost, I turned to God to show me the way.

I learned to have patience with myself, and I urge you to give yourself that gift too. If you've been lame for a long time, you have to build up your strength. Just like working out, it's going to take time to strengthen those muscles.

My advice is when you have setbacks, do not let yourself stop or get stuck. Don't beat yourself up, or focus on it, dust yourself off and keep going. The only way through this, my friends, is through it.

One step. Two steps. Three steps… and on.

I hope and pray that you will never doubt healing is possible. I'm not unique. If it was for me, it is for you, too. Against all odds, and despite the path my life took, I am here.

Today, the ashes of my past have become a beautiful gift I can give to you.

God has taken the burned and dirty ashes from my past and created something new. He showed me how to trust, and love, and live in and through Him.

Now it's your turn. You are right where you need to be, and it is the right time. Friend, I ask you, "Do you want to be healed?"

Stand up and walk.

Questions

1. Name the things in your life, that you most want God to change. How would it change your life, if that one thing changed?

2. What dream, hope, or desire is most difficult to believe God can provide? Why?

3. How will healing from your "lameness" change your life? What would be the greatest impact?

CONCLUSION

Butterflies are fascinating.

If you ever study them, you'll find out they go through many stages in their lives. The last one involves being locked away in a cocoon where they are changed inside and out, and they experience a complete transformation.

It's absolutely amazing, and the best part is how they emerge from the process. When the change is complete, the butterfly must fight to escape their cocoon.

This part of their journey is difficult, and if you're watching them try to get out, it can be tempting to help them by cutting away the cocoon. But, don't! You see, the butterfly must struggle, and push their way out. Without the struggle, the butterfly will never fly.

In many ways, our own our journey from pain and ashes to beauty and restoration is like the journey of a butterfly. Often, it's the struggle that leads us to being able to fly.

As God restored the identity He created for me alone, I began to spread my own wings. I started to embrace many of the things I used to hide away, like art, music, and writing. And as part of that creative spirit He gave me, I developed a hobby refurbishing old and shabby furniture. The more broken down, the better!

I'd redone a few pieces when I realized there was actually beauty in the chipping, peeling paint that covered many of the pieces. To me, it was the dings and marks that gave them character. So, I stopped painting and fixing, and just loved them as is.

In traditional Japanese aesthetics, this is referred to as wabi-sabi or wobi-sobi.

Wabi-sabi is an acceptance of imperfection. It's a fascinating art form, and I rather love the imagery it implies. I too have come to believe there is great beauty in things (and people) that are less than perfect.

Here's the thing, friends. We are never going to reach a state of perfection on this side of heaven. God wants us to move past the lameness that keeps us stuck. He doesn't want us laying on mats year after year – always hoping, but never changing.

God can restore that part of us. But, know this. Even when we've done the work and reached a better place, there will always be more to restore because we are at our best, messy.

This book is not the whole process. It's only a place to begin; a starting point. Restoration and healing are a journey, not a destination.

Still, I want you to embrace the journey, and I'd love to walk alongside you on the way.

My hope and prayer are that this book will inspire you to begin, and continue to let God heal and transform you.

Will you stand up and walk with me?

ABOUT THE AUTHOR

Shelley is an author, speaker, and mentor who uses her life experiences to help individuals recognize and pursue their God-given purpose and identity. She has a heart for people – especially those broken and held captive by difficult past experiences.

After years of struggling with a painful history of sexual, verbal, and physical abuse, she found healing through faith. The insights gained through her restoration journey, along with her passion for helping others find freedom from past difficulties, became the foundation for her writing and ministry.

Her transformation story is remarkable and she inspires others through speaking, writing, blogging, and poetry.

Follow her on all social media platforms or on her website at:

www.shelleyfurtadolinton.com